SPELL BOOK

A Comprehensive Guide to
Magic Spells and Incantations
(2023 Beginner Crash Course)

Abby Flowers

Contents

Introduction

As much as contemporary occultism attempts to shed light on diverse subjects, Some topics remain inexorably related to superstition, which, when ignored, tarnishes the dignity of activities with origins in historical settings that are completely different from how widespread mystification characterizes them. Vodou and Hoodoo are two arguments that suffer the most from this mentality. Not only are the terms used interchangeably, even though they don't mean the same thing, but they are also linked to scary images from movies and TV shows and are thought to be the source of all evil. This is why many people say you shouldn't do these things without a proper understanding or knowledge, either theoretical or practical.

Curses, love and separation ceremonies, ligaments, fetishes, animal sacrifices, and everything else bad that is associated with Vodou and Hoodoo are all things that can be found at any time and place, in any religion, type of magic, or society, but with different dynamics. No civilization has been spared from them, not even Europe, which is so proud of its superiority in terms of civilization and ethics and is higher and fairer than that of the "African savages." This way of thinking, which tends to dismiss anything from Africa or "primitive" countries, did not end when slavery ended. On the contrary, it remains anchored and, in some ways, is expanding under the strain of progressive media indoctrination, which drives people to see anything else as inferior. On the other hand, cultural poverty discourages any in-depth study, not just of the fields listed and the anthropological foundations on which they are based, but also of the bare minimum of general culture needed to understand the world. Functional illiteracy, which is a big problem for academic books, is spreading more and more. This makes it hard for many people to tell the difference between reality and fiction, so they believe everything they see on TV, even if it's just for fun, instead of using their critical thinking skills to find out the truth. In this way, incorrect stereotypes take hold, leading some to see Vodou as a collection of blood sacrifices, curses, and dolls capable of wreaking all kinds of evil. People on the esoteric web are no different: Vodou is often discouraged because it is dangerous and focuses on worshiping a pantheon of only evil entities. Other times, it is recommended as the only way to make death and destruction spells work, or it is said to be old-fashioned and based on primitive religion.

It is a series of the worst clichés, concealing just a vast ignorance and dread of anything unfamiliar and personally different.

First and foremost, a distinction must be made between Hoodoo and Vodou, with the former being nothing more than a form of folk magic practiced throughout the American continent, from north to south, that incorporates European elements alongside those of African-American, Native American, and Oriental origin (consider the role of Chinese pierced coins used as amulets). Hoodoo, as a sort of folk magic, is anchored at a popular level, even among individuals who are not full-fledged esotericists, and is unrelated to any religion. There are no reference gods, no religious hierarchy, and no persons who assume the function of priests. Rootworkers are Hoodoo specialists, although they do not perform priestly duties.

On the other hand, Vodou is a religion in its own right, with its own religious organization, clergy, liturgy, and well-defined orthopraxy. It is also an initiatory religion, passed down via communities whose members belong to a particular House, which maintains track of all generations to assure the cult's suitable transmission and the initiatory lineage of its priests. The Vodou religion shows a lot of things, one of which is that its pantheon can't be made up of only bad spirits. Even the Ghedé, the gods associated with death, play protective roles while also encouraging the passage. As the most extreme form of the creative drive, the Rada can also have bad and destructive effects (see Legba, who is both the messenger and the warrior, and sometimes even the trickster, depending on the situation and need). The Petro are vengeful gods who punish wrongdoers. They also represent the spirit of survival, rebellion, and longing for freedom that slaves felt during their time in captivity (this is a reference to the Slave Trade, which began in 1790 and ended after 1900).

The Vodou, like other faiths, has its magical component, which is nothing more than the supernatural manifestation in human life, the irruption of good or malicious, divine or demonic energies into the world when summoned by priests or sorcerers. No human community, whether European or African, is hungry just for destruction and death. The demands of existence are as many as the reasons why the art of the spell was and continues to be practiced today. Love, barrier removal, wealth, blessing, healing, divination, and war—everything required for a man to live, thrive, and better his situation has its magical manifestation, which is grounded in the expression of religion.

Concerning the infamous voodoo dolls, it is important to note that making fetishes that look like people is not unique to Vodou. It is common in many cultures, and there are many examples, even from Europe, of fetishes that heal or help people fall in love instead of killing or cursing. The main concept is to build a simulacrum of the person, connect it to it via witnesses (bodily fluids, hair, nails, personal effects, simple images, and so on), and then baptize and animate it so that what is done on the fetish occurs on the person via sympathetic magic.

The uniqueness of voodoo and hoodoo dolls is that plants or other substances are sometimes inserted within them in addition to witnesses and padding. The fetish is stimulated by needles (which are sometimes ritualized themselves), which are pierced in various locations to produce specific effects (the heart is hit for love spells or removal, the pubis for fertility or sterility, the sick part for disease healing, the head for instilling ideas, and so on). In this regard, the procedure varies from that of Europe, where the simulacra were generally made of wax, baptized, etched with spells, and then buried.

Finally, the most disturbing and offensive idea is to attribute any strangeness to the Vodou: it brings greasy feces in front of the house, dead animals, strange symbols, anything that causes disquiet and exiles from the knowledge of popular magic automatically becomes "a curse made by those of the Vodou," as if they were a mafia, and, once again, without making a proper distinction with Hoodoo. Both use ritual oils, powders, and water (colonies), but most of the time, it's to dress candles, do ritual baths or ablutions, or put on the body. The procedure rarely includes leaving striking indications of magical work on someone since it would be like alerting him that something has been done, which is not a very smart decision. On the other hand, in Italian folk magic, leaving striking remnants is common practice, frequently utilized not for magical objectives but to terrify your opponent pragmatically (also, the fear that someone has already cast a spell helps it go halfway, owing to the gap left by dread).

As usual, the suggestion is to record yourself before succumbing to clichés. On the one side, to lessen the needless fear of Vodou, and on the other, to understand how to discern and interpret the various practices, knowing how to protect oneself or employ them in case of necessity. Culture is always the key to understanding the

world in all of its parts, and it's the only way to bring
people together without mistrust or fear but with the
right amount of respect.

The aim of this book

This book discusses hoodoo, a popular kind of magic created among the African-American community in the American South. This type of magic has strong influences from Africa, Europe, and Native America, giving it a strong syncretic flavor.

From a historical standpoint, most hoodoo practitioners are Afro-American; individuals who follow and practice this magic are known as rootworkers or root physicians, albeit root working, i.e., magical work with herbs and roots, is simply a subset of this magic system.

Hoodoo originated among African slaves in the United States, and signs of its existence have been discovered in states such as Alabama, Georgia, Louisiana, Arkansas, Florida, and Mississippi, as well as South Carolina, North Carolina, Virginia, Tennessee, and Illinois.

It is important to note that Hoodoo is neither a religion nor a magical system associated with any one faith, even if its practitioners are Christian. Hoodoo physicians used to be nomadic, traveling from city to city and teaching their wisdom. Hoodoo is not a magical system restricted to a select few initiates since some of its fundamental methods are now part of the folklore heritage of several African American civilizations, mainly in the south of the United States.

Among the numerous magic systems from which Hoodoo has drawn is also the European and Euro-American magic heritage, which has exerted its influence via its grimoires, notably through the grimoire "sixth and seventh book of Moses."

Hoodoo incorporates various Hebrew symbols and seals connected to Moses' power to perform miracles employed by hoodoo practitioners without following specific processes.

What exactly is Hoodoo?

Hoodoo (pron. Udu) has an unknown origin, although it is nearly definitely African. In the United States, it refers to a wide range of superstitious magical rituals and African-American origin beliefs. Conjure man, hoodoo man, and root doctor are terms used to describe the ceremonies and prayers associated with these beliefs. Hoodoo is envisioned as a collection of legends, "sympathetic" and "non-sympathetic" practices, elementary Kabbalah, traditional herbalist treatments, and a successful synthesis of traditional folk magic with origins in Africa and development in the late-seventeenth-century enslaved environments of African Americans. It's hard to know how far these ideas and activities have spread because the word "hoodoo" can mean anything from elemental ceremony magic to making amulets. What is clear is that hoodoo is primarily practiced in the New Orleans region. Even if they don't say it aloud, these ideas pervade the Protestant sector of American culture. A few million people from all walks of life agree with these points of view.

Hoodoo is sometimes associated with religion, yet it seldom has a defined religious meaning. There are no specific divinities or defined theologies to whom a hoodoo practitioner or devotee relates. Religion is introduced through exclusion in Hoodoo. It fills a need that orthodox belief cannot fill because it is too speculative.

Images of Catholic saints, Buddhists, pagan deities, and figures having more to do with superstition than the holy, folklore symbols, and occasionally an altar that is merely a patchwork of religious conflicts may be seen on practitioners' altars. Along with pictures of Catholic saints, including St. Espedito, St. Photinus, St. Mary, and St. Anthony, there are representations of Shiva, Kali, Bhudda, Mercury, and others... All of this, in any event, is irrelevant to the practitioner on duty, whose prayers and dedications are primarily directed at the spirits of the deceased and natural spirits, neither of which has a special significance. It may seem unusual, but it is not if we consider the core of Hoodoo, which is the pursuit of worldly benefits via magic. Whatever sign, item, or ritual the practitioner employs is simply meant as a means to a goal, and this aim is quite clear. The purpose justifies the means in Hoodoo. Hoodoo has undergone the most diverse influences that have grafted on to a base indeed African, then changing rituals and materials from European magic, Catholicism, Native American beliefs, and finally, but only after the abolition of slavery, from African-American religions such as voodoo, the pole, santeria, and macuba. The rituals are primarily personal in nature. As a result, there are no group rituals in this setting; instead, the practitioner works alone. Except when he wishes to convey his knowledge or when the ritual necessitates additional presence, his connection with the spirits is fundamentally personal.

What does not constitute hoodoo?

First and foremost, hoodoo is not a religion. Hoodoo is not even considered a religion. It is often mistaken for voodoo in Europe and other superficial settings. As we shall see, hoodoo and voodoo are fundamentally distinct and far apart in origin and environment. Voodoo is a Fon and Guinean religion that is very good at magic rituals, especially in the Caribbean countries of Haiti (where it is called "authentic voodoo") and Santo Domingo (where it has a different meaning known as the "12 divisions"). Voodoo is heavily influenced by Catholicism and contains a pantheon of divinities known as loa or lwa, each with a specific meaning related to a simple picture of certain Catholic saints. There is also, and it cannot be otherwise, a well-organized hierarchical scale and social rituals, whether public or private, in which each individual has their position and role, which are then mirrored in society. The rites are directed by the houngan (priest) or mambo (priestess); the cuisiniere prepares the sacrifices to the loa; Sur Pwan, Hounsi Kanzo, and Hounsi Ventalleur are some of the titles that the vuduisant (voodoo practitioner) adopts in the voodoo temple hierarchy.

There is a chorus for the songs, there are powerful symbols, temples and special symbols, and certain initiations that the faithful must go through to ascend the hierarchy. This must be seen in Hoodoo, which lacks initiation, degrees, social rites, and public temples. On the surface, there is a similarity in vocabulary (for example, the hoodoo practitioner may employ voodoo loa pictures), but the commonality of terms ends there. Other Afro-Caribbean faiths, such as santeria, candomble, palo, batuque, umbanda, and quimbanda, are similar. Some simply stem from other traditions and have been merged with others at various periods and locations. However, almost all of these religions have a hierarchy, initiatory degrees, terminologies, and unique theologies, which elevates them to the status of "state religions" (such as voodoo in Haiti); this is not seen in hoodoo, where all this is essentially useless.

History

Before we go into the history of hoodoo, certain explanations are needed. To begin with, it is difficult to give specific facts and dates while researching the origins and history of folklore rituals and traditional religions, and hoodoo is no exception. The chronological sequence and testimony in these situations are virtually invariably based on facts and stories passed down orally for generations by individuals who have never been exposed to the scientific approach. As a result, we shall depend on language assonances and etymologies of popular terminology, on a few particular occurrences that happened throughout formative eras, on the testimony of newspapers and field academics, and, of course, on tales. However, this is often the least dependable aspect of our study. First, we will define "hoodoo." As previously said, its etymology is unknown. Some academics associate it with the Guinean word voodoo or vodun, which means "mystery" and often refers to the spirits worshiped in the voodoo pantheon. The similarities between the two terminologies, however, stop here since the methodologies and structures of the two traditions are fundamentally different from the facts previously stated in earlier chapters. However, some practitioners attribute the name hoodoo back to the mispronounced Hispanic judio (i.e., "Jew") phrase used to stigmatize black magic techniques.

The Senegalese names gris-gris and ju-ju, which mean "amulet" or "good luck charm," are often employed. Then there's "mojo," which might be derived from the Yoruba word "mojuba" (prayer). Finally, the "deadly dust" employed in hoodoo is termed "goofer dust"; the phrase "goofer" appears to be a variation of the Congolese term "kufwa" which means "death." We can discern the multiple effects the practice has had throughout time by analyzing the terms, but not their origin. We will then need to refer to other information. First and foremost, we know that hoodoo is unquestionably of African origin. As a result, we must examine the history of American slavery, which lasted from 1619 to 1865. During this time, roughly twelve million people were removed from the west coast of Africa and transported to the east coast of the American continent. For practical reasons, it was often desirable to keep the ethnic groupings to which they belonged. As a result, there was a predominant divide based on nations and vocations, i.e., the majority of the enslaved people were typical of one ethnic group. The Yoruba strain, which founded the Candomblè heritage, was enslaved in Brazil. The Yoruba established Santeria in Cuba, while the Congo strain generated Palo Mayombe. The Dahomey strain gave rise to Voodoo in Haiti and St. Domingo. Obeah was born in Jamaica as a result of the Ashanti custom.

Finally, all of these traditions started to borrow vocabulary and ideas from Western traditions, and the spirits of Voodoo and Santeria were identified with Catholic saints. The strains implicated in New Orleans and the southern United States were mostly Congo and Senegal. Proof of this is that the space in New Orleans where slaves used to meet to dance was named "Congo square" until a century ago, in the same manner, that the Italian district was dubbed "Little Palermo."

The sorts of ceremonies associated with hoodoo support the notion of Congo and Senegalese origin. There is a longstanding history in Senegal of "marabouts," uninitiated sorcerers who address divine issues by prescribing amulets, roots, and traditional herbal treatments. In Congo, the worship of the dead is vital, and familiar is the usage of containers with more or less strong values depending on the content, which may range from the amulet to the actual "container for spirits." These many traditions may be seen in the figures of the root doctor (hoodoo practitioner), the use of mojo bags (which, as we shall learn later, are unique amulets considered "living"), and the intricate considerations surrounding the voodoo box (in any case a more modern instrument). It has been said multiple times that the original slave hoodoo started to mingle with various foreign customs throughout time. Today, two major superstitions are separated into believers and practitioners, demonstrating Afro-European syncretism.

The first is of African origin and is known as "live things in you." It is primarily held by the African American population. It corresponds to the belief that a sorcerer could populate the body of an unfortunate man with swarms of animals, whether snakes, frogs, spiders, or not better identified "puppets," through various means. The second is of European origin and is mostly regarded by the Mediterranean strain's people. It believes in the evil eye or that an envious person may curse another person via the eye, even by coincidence. Hoodoo, on the other hand, has not only taken but also given a lot over its history. Being the practitioners and believers for 80% of the African-American strain population, the practice has infiltrated and continues to permeate a portion of their existence. There are allusions to this throughout art, music, and culture. Music, in particular, has had the largest impact, somehow tied to that personal and almost hallowed dimension also affected by hoodoo. When you listen to the blues, you will hear words like mojo, goofer dust, the devil, the black man, and references to love and hate spells; many of the blues stories (one in particular) are the stories of musicians who have influenced music for decades and are stories about suffering, misery, and hoodoo. It is not always simple to locate references, but those who are familiar with the topic are clear and evident. Candle rituals have now expanded across 'esotericism.' They are similar, if not slightly modified, to those employed by the conjure man of the early and middle '900, and fortunate charms and rituals that have spread throughout America and now even in Europe have their origins in New Orleans. Hoodoo has a short history with few dates and many nearly legendary facts; the practice is so ubiquitous and interwoven into a society that it is practically undetectable.

Hoodoo Society

The typical society in which hoodoo is born is unquestionably one of low-medium extraction, even if its activities may be found at all socioeconomic levels.

It is a culture built on everyday problems, frequently based on ignorance and based on faith out of need. However, it would be incorrect to claim that hoodoo activities result only from irrational beliefs. This dimension undoubtedly exists, as it does in religion, but hoodoo is now employed for "reasoned faith" and naive popular absorption. Folklore and the anthropological side of the practice have been written about in the past century, and more serious studies are being done on the topic. Many persons who have experienced "high" esotericism turn to hoodoo practice because the benefits are undeniable. No official initiations to go through, no costly equipment to purchase, and no "special" venues are required to function. Each ceremony is straightforward, straightforward, and nearly usually adaptable at will. This makes hoodoo a road that anybody can travel without trouble, without being bound to groups of unknown practitioners, just by recording and experimenting. In this scenario, the Internet comes in handy. On the Internet, you can easily contact practitioners who are eager to assist you; on specialized sites, you can purchase exotic materials, find treatises, traditional and non-traditional books, and even take correspondence courses on tradition and practice, aided by periodic examinations and online assistance. The entire procedure may seem ridiculous, but it has little effect on the aspiring root doctor's competence or sensitivity since hoodoo is more concerned with the outcome than theory.

However, among all the tough and intricate issues of sociality, there are some intriguing "social groups," such as the spiritualist church. In the southern United States, the connection between hoodoo and the spiritualist religion is widely recognized and fairly strong. The spiritualist church was founded in England in the middle of the nineteenth century by the spiritualist movement, which promotes contact with spirits via mediums. The spiritualist church believes in the existence of a spiritual realm where men's souls go after death and with whom one may communicate via trained persons known as "mediums," or "mezzo" in Latin. Spiritualist churches are common in Anglo-Saxon nations; the liturgy is unique and comprises an opening prayer, devoted prayers, songs, and eventually, a mediumistic demonstration, in which the medium summons various spirits who converse with those who attend the cult via him or her. They are often referred to be the ghosts of devoted relatives or friends. The medium is taught to provide clear descriptions to prove that the contacted ghost is who he claims to be. Hoodoo practitioners will discover in this style of the church all of the ingredients necessary for their worship, particularly communication with spirits and worship of the dead. There is no genuine requirement to join a religious organization or group to be a two-headed doctor unless you have an extremely conservative social view.

The Root Doctor

A root doctor, the practitioner or hoodoo practitioner, is someone who is well-versed in the rituals, materials, and hoodoo heritage. The term "root doctor" refers to a doctor who treats roots. Probably because herbs and roots were employed as herbalist remedies in addition to orthodox medicine. Hoodoo man, hoodoo lady, conjure man, or conjure woman are other names for it. Another term for him is "two-headed doctors" or "twoheaded doctor," which may reflect the dual nature of his profession in that he may fix or cause issues. The virtually honorary titles of mama (mom), dad (dad), uncle (uncle), hount (aunt), or doctor are sometimes attached to the actual name. Typically, a well-integrated community member can live off his practices as if they were regular employment; his authority in issues of "trouble resolution," significant or tiny, is acknowledged and utilized. He has relationships with the local religious cult, particularly in areas where Christian spiritualist communities are established; the various ministers of worship frequently do not approve of hoodoo practice but rarely publicly oppose it because the community is very attached to it and the root doctor is generally a faithful assiduous or otherwise does not disdain the official cult. The root doctor is said to be "possessed by spirits," implying that he has deep knowledge of the spirit realm. It refers to him (or her) asserting that he or she can "place a straight lick with a crooked stick" (in the original meaning "put a straight lick with a crooked stick") or that he or she "has the talent," or even that he or she "is marked." The "gift" or "sign" is uniquely determined by certain circumstances at birth. Assume the unborn kid is breech, is delivered wrapped in a portion of an amniotic sack, is the survivor of twins, is the seventh child of a seventh child, or is resuscitated shortly after birth. In such a situation, it is believed that the gift marks the occasion, similar to what occurs in many places of the globe, including Italy. Another form of being "marked" is to survive a lightning strike, coma, or apparent death. In any event, not all "marked" are conjure men, and not all "marked" are conjure men. The twoheaded doctor has a unique position in the societal imagination. The priest comes into touch with the holy by vocation, while the root doctor comes into contact with the sacred by inclination.

Books about Magic

First, we will discuss the most widely utilized book in the world: the Bible.

The Bible is regarded as "the greatest of the magical texts" by many conjured men. Conjure man has some pretty strange views of the interpretation of the passages and principles of the Bible, in addition to employing invocations and passages from the Bible (particularly the Old Testament) as magic formulae. The psalms are definitely the most utilized passages; there are 150 of them, and each one is associated with a distinct efficacy in the realm of magic by the root doctor. There are psalms for safe travel, psalms for protection, psalms for consecration, psalms to drive away or strike the adversary, psalms for love, gambling, and so on. They are so utilized that some contemporary conjurers created particular treatises on the topic, for example, the renowned "power of the psalms" by Godfrey Selig. As a result, the Bible is regarded as a massive dissertation on hoodoo. God is seen as the most excellent root doctor, and the cosmos' creation is a magnificent piece of magic. People have the right to conduct hoodoo and magic since God gives man the ability to name (and so command) all animals. Furthermore, since God punishes, blesses, aids, or curses, and because he knows and foresees everything, why shouldn't this punishment or blessing flow via the hands of the conjure man, so making him a divine instrument? Moses is regarded as a powerful conjurer, and two apocryphal volumes utilized by root workers, the sixth and seventh books of Moses, are credited to him (actually two grimoires, probably Renaissance). So how can we explain the Mosaic Law's restriction against magic? Simple: Moses prohibited regular people from practicing hoodoo, reserving it for the priestly elite. Although it may seem unusual, scriptural quotations back up these arguments and interpretations. We may provide some instances of "biblical hoodoo" legends, as described by the great root-worker Doctor Kioni:

In Genesis 30:1,43, Jacob gives the white sheep water by putting debarked and processed sticks in the water, causing the sheep to give birth to stuffed children instead of white ones; in the first book of Samuel 30:7,20, king David asks God for a response, and he answers through the stones of the priest's breastplate (which is said to be a work of divination today); and

in the book of Numbers 5:11,31, it is said that To find out whether a wife has been betrayed, go to the priest, who will have her drink consecrated water with dust taken from the tabernacle and curse the water, so that if the lady has been deceived, she will also be cursed.

These are not the only instances; the Bible is replete of these "approved hoodoo deeds," even though Mosaic law forbids them. The barrier between magical ritual and religious ritual, on the other hand, is often dissolved; beyond the meanings and authorizations, the magician thinks himself a priest and behaves accordingly.

The root doctor's interpretation may be motivated by convenience, but it is not without support in the text. Other books often employed by the hoodoo man include the sixth and seventh books of Moses, two grimoires of hazy biblical origin that are little more than catalogs of formulae and ready-to-use magic pictures inspired by Moses' activities, interpreted as hoodoo acts. In this section, we will uncover the formulae that Moses used to vanquish the Egyptian magicians in the well-known tale. He sent down a hailstorm and even a handful of formulations that claim to make God appear in person before people who repeat them (!). The grimoire "powwow or the long lost companion" is another text. A collection of prayers and formulae of Central European provenance was almost definitely carried to America by the Dutch community towards the end of the nineteenth century.

Some formulations should cure common ills (worms, bruises, and wounds) and protect against evil, bad spirits, and bad luck. In actuality, the conjure man often does not utilize the formulae for the deeds described in the scriptures but instead adapts them to his situation, as he does with the psalms. Moses' formula against Egyptian magicians may be used to defeat an adversary, the hail formula to kill him, and the divine apparition formula to bless plants and preparations. As a result, there is once again a big deal of flexibility in practice, aided by basically conventional operating principles.

In certain circumstances, the book serves as an authentic amulet (powwows also serve this purpose) or is used to ward off evil spirits (for example, you leave the Bible open at a specific page on the altar, pointing it in a specific direction). Some other additional books and pamphlets may be employed in the practice of hoodoo; analyzing them all would be beyond the scope of this dissertation, not to mention practically impossible. Consider that, in addition to traditional, regional, and imported publications, books created from the ground up by today's conjure man are utilized.

CHAPTER 1

Hoodoo Magic Elements

Hoodoo is founded on basic concepts, as has been stated countless times. These are fundamentally two principles: tradition and sympathetic magic. As for tradition, we have already discussed it in history and will do so again. Today, we want to talk about the idea of sympathetic magic and, more importantly, how hoodoo works. It has previously been said that there is some leeway in interpretation; nevertheless, this does not imply that the conjure man performs everything that comes to mind. There are different versions of each ritual, combination, and prayer. It's up to the rootworker to choose the best one or "construct" (not make, but pay attention to) an equal version based on the same principles.

So we would argue that sympathetic magic is basically built on assonances, and its foundation premise is "the like attracts the like." Whether the parallels are in form, thought, or behavior, it makes no difference. So, in hoodoo, there are rituals that look like the things the root worker wants to happen, herbs and things that have shapes that match a thought, and prayers that talk about the subject of the spell they are used for.

We use dolls baptized with the name of the person you want to heal or curse, for example; single magnetic stones attract luck, matched in pairs attract love; dice bring luck to the game; violets, which resemble a heart in shape, are used in love spells; white candles are used to bless, red candles for sexual spells, and green candles for money spells (American dollars are all green). Some connections that have been around for a long time but have lost their original meaning are harder to understand.

Why does a tooth, an alligator, or a rabbit's foot bring good luck in gambling? What role does a horseshoe play in bringing good luck? Why is the hardened gambler carrying a horse chestnut fruit? In some cases, historians will be able to provide some vague and uncertain elucidation, such as in the case of horseshoes, where they can tell us that in Roman times some of them were made of silver, and finding one was undoubtedly a stroke of luck, but what about cinnamon, used for both love and money, or beans that help prevent the evil eye?

All of these ideas and elements help to give hoodoo its distinct and recognized taste worldwide, even when the traditional rites are employed to aid other ideologies or even other faiths. When people talk about this on mailing lists, some of them often wonder if the ritual that Wiccans use instead of chaos magick comes from hoodoo or not. In her excellent book "Hoodoo Rootwork Correspondence Course," Catherine Yronwode offers a very simple and very suitable comparison of hoodoo to cookery. A person who understands the taste of a specific style of the dish will recognize it everywhere. There may be hundreds of variants, spices, and condiments, but the appearance and scent of that cuisine will stay consistent.

On the contrary, you will notice if any element is out of place right away. Tacos with guacamole sauce are not served during a traditional Tuscan supper. Similarly, a traditional ceremony in which candles are transported from day to day to bring two lovers together is identifiable as hoodoo, even if performed by a Wicca practitioner in the Siberian Arctic. Let us now delve into further depth and explore the familiar hoodoo surroundings and core ideas.

The cemetery

This brings us to a susceptible subject inside our company.

If understanding the development environment and hoodoo history is simple, understanding the practice environment is more complicated. The first one we'll look at is one that everyone is familiar with, but it elicits mixed feelings: the cemetery.

There are many hoodoo spells and rituals that involve going to the cemetery. To avoid getting into dark topics, we'll talk about the severe limits that can be reached in the job of a root doctor. At the very least, you can pray at the cemetery or use a small amount of cemetery soil (usually a few grams) from the outside of certain graves to make amulets and powders. The most you can do is place votive lights on a grave or bury a little fetish on the side. Another old technique is to make amulets out of human bones or teeth.

Human bones may be securely obtained from businesses specializing in anatomical models, which can give the components separately or transport complete skeletons, mounted with appropriate attachments, to researchers, painters, or anatomy aficionados, in Anglo-Saxon nations. It is intriguing to consider that although many people worry about the bones of destitute animals, no one blinks an eye when nameless skeletons of strangers who died in China or India are sold piece by piece. Lupus in Homo Homini. However, although it was formerly possible to utilize their own extinct ashes or to purchase a little bone part from a complacent cemetery keeper, the practice is now much less common. However, in Italy, all of this is illegal under current legislation; thus, we will not explain any amulet that incorporates such things.

I promise you that what does not seem to be a "moral restriction" is, and it is, an exception among Afro-Caribbean and Afro-American customs, some of which regard extinct loved ones in quite different ways. Concerning other cemetery customs, we shall discuss just the most basic, which is equally fundamental in hoodoo: "buying land" in the cemetery, land that can now be purchased in specialist shops.

Obviously, this acquaintance with death and the dead shocks or shakes the most sensitive minds. On the other hand, the psychology of the root doctor is considerably different from that of the average, well, thinking person. The conjure man does not regard the graveyard as a location of ancestral dread and "evil ideas," but rather as a place of life and, particularly, holy power. It is a space for a different way of life, with which one may relate, enjoy, and which is often "familiar" in the genuine meaning of the term. The root doctor thinks that the person who died is still alive and well and can take care of what they have to offer on their own. It may appear absurd to those accustomed to the reverent fear of earthly remains. Still, the Tibetan Buddhist monk who serves the Buddha drinks in human skull cups or blows during ceremonies in flutes made from the shins of old llamas does not differ from conjure man; he does much more, except that he is generally more sympathetic to public opinion due to his peaceful demeanor.

The crossroads and the black man.

The crossroads is another well-known location in the art of hoodoo. The "X" intersection, in particular, has significant significance. It is the world's center, the point from which all highways go and from which all corners of the globe can be viewed. It is an exceptional ceremonial location, filled with power and inhabited by strong spirits.

A lot of people in ancient Europe were interested in this, which put the newsstands of the family lari and the god Mercury at a crossroads. These newsstands later became the Italian madonnas and saints. The Madonna or Saint has most likely been present since the year 500, while the newsstand has most likely been there since 300 before Christ. The hoodoo crossroads is the topic of folklore, pacts with the spirits, and the preferred haunt of a particular character: the black man. He is sometimes mistaken for the Devil and is also known as the Devil or

Satan, although root doctors know there is nothing more distinct. The black man, or man of the crossroads, is an iconic figure seen in many civilizations across the globe, particularly in African religions and rituals and those that stem from them. Exu, eleggua, papa legba, maitre carrefour, calfu, and lucero world are just a few of his monikers. He is a god in some faiths and philosophies, an ancestor with immense abilities in others, but he is always associated with four things: change, crossing, divination, and play. He is seen as a joker spirit, a lover of parties and gambling, who likes telling jokes, and is often regarded as the connector between the gods and man.

It is honored and offered before the other spirits, and in the hoodoo, it is the only spirit with a specialized ritual, the crossing ceremony, which permits the person who performs it to create a deal with him. This agreement gives good fortune to people who sign it and may be utilized to gain renown or talent. What makes this spirit more profound and more intriguing is that it never resists a desire, no matter what kind it is. It is the encounter with our inner unconscious, the unspoken longing, and our genuine moral core. The crossroads and the black guy are just observed; they cannot be explained. Here the gnosis, the divine intuition, and the individual's unique sensitivity come into play.

Spirits

Spirits are the cornerstone of hoodoo, one of the few "strong" beliefs present, and one of the sines qua non-prerequisites for hoodoo to become an act without a rational basis. Spirits are the souls of the dead, associated with deeds, people, and places, but seldom with a precise meaning. The easiest way to define hoodoo spirits is to look at the laws that govern them. In truth, like the living, they are subject to strict constraints according to tradition.

They affect and control daily life; they are a member of human society, and they move and act with specific goals and wants that are comparable to those of the living. So a spirit will be unable to cross a bridge, a live watercourse (such as a river), a busy road, or certain "magic" obstacles (such as lines of brick or white salt dust or spots where special prayers have been spoken) until the root doctor eliminates these barriers by his magic. Spirits cannot enter a home unless summoned from inside. They will be lured in by certain invocations, prayers, and artifacts, then driven out and exorcised by similar invocations, prayers, and objects. They will appreciate money, candles, food, chile, and pepper, but they will despise salt and will demand payment for every service done, so much so that they will take a payment due if it is not paid.

The most intriguing aspect of hoodoo is that ghosts may come to life and become real. There are many urban legends about people who never existed: the old woman who prays on the grave that turns out to be hers; the clerk who gives in change a lucky coin, but then no one remembers; the little man with the red hat who asks the root doctor why he collects a grass, who says he has always lived there, but no one knows or remembers. Of course, it is reasonable to explain all of these events with coincidences and the proliferation of urban legends. However, in hoodoo, logic takes on a fascinating meaning, a halo of mystery that adds to producing that specific taste, that impression of an unseen and ever-present company, that specific humorous and macabre atmosphere of something just beyond the border, so close that you can touch it.

A crossing is any location where two highways meet and create a cross with the same arms as the plus sign. Crossroads are the meeting points of the realm of man and the kingdom of the spirit. As a result, they belong to everyone and no one. Some people categorize crosses as masculine or female. Male crosses are the three intersecting lines that make a capital T, with the three points symbolizing the penis and testicles. Female crosses are four-way crosses that are claimed to depict the inner and outer vaginal lip.

They are said to be very powerful, and as such, they are often used to execute spells and rituals, put offerings, and dispose of finished spells. For example, after having a spiritual cleansing bath, individuals often dispose of part of their spent bath water at a crossroads to spread the negative influence that has been washed away. Similarly, the leftovers of finished spells, such as awakening candles, are placed at a crossroads, sometimes in a paper bag, and sometimes buried nearby.

The soil from the crossroads is often gathered and utilized in spells. For example, a recipe for wooing a male lover calls for dirt from a three-way intersection. In other circumstances, you may utilize the crossroads to convince someone to leave you by taking the soil from their footprint and dusting a pinch or two in their shoes, then at each crossroads between their house and the city borders.

The Ritual of the Crossroads

Many cultures associate the crossroads with witchcraft and sorcery, as well as beings like Hecate, Mercury, Ellegua, Ganesh, Pope Legba, St. Peter, and the Devil. The Devil at the Crossroads, also known as the Black Man, is not the antagonist described in the Christian Bible but rather a generous spirit who struggled with Satan when African slaves were compelled to adopt Christianity.

Many of these spiritual creatures are recognized for their power over both the living and the dead and their capacity to freely traverse between realms, eliminate barriers, remove conditions crossed, and open the way. The most well-known (but often misunderstood) rite of the crossroads is meeting the Devil at the crossroads to become an expert in a certain task.

Several versions of the Crossroads Ritual may be found in "Hoodoo, Spell, Sorcery, Witchcraft, Basic Work," a folklore collection compiled by retired Anglican pastor Harry Middleton Hyatt between 1935 and 1939. The majority of the ceremonies follow a general structure with occasional variations (e.g., time of day, number of days, etc.).

To perform the Crossroads Ritual, bring the true item you desire to master to the crossroads at midnight for 9 nights in a row. Bring a deck of Tarot cards, for example, if you want to enhance your card reading; sew a whole magic hand for 9 nights in a row if you want to become a master at making magic hands.

You may or may not observe or be welcomed by any number of black creatures while visiting the crossroads every night. A figure will welcome you on the last night. It may be a person clothed in black, or it could be a black guy (i.e., a person of African heritage), but it will be the

Devil. If you don't exhibit any fear, he'll take the thing you've brought to him and teach you how to utilize it properly. Finally, he will return the thing to you, and you will have mastery and the capacity to utilize it.

Divination

Divination is an essential component of root working. There is no established understanding in "new age" usage that the items used for divination are just a medium by which the unconscious interprets the replies or even a form of "meditative mandala" in these activities. On the other hand, there is not even a notion analogous to the superstitious European view according to which the things in \squestion speak being endowed with some "power." Instead, any item or method employed in hoodoo for divination is considered a form of spiritual expression. Spirits communicate via cards, shells, ouija boards, bones, domino.... tiles, and less often by the mere possession of a medium. The ways and things employed are the most diverse; here is a short rundown of the most frequent and oddest.

The deck of cards is the most frequently utilized item by the conjureman. Usually a plain deck of 40 cards or a deck of gypsy cards (like our "sibyls"), much less often the tarot, which struggles to gain traction in rural culture.

Another typical method is the pendulum, which is often in the shape of a "jack ball," a wax ball packed with herbs ideal for divination and strung on a rope and maintained with the same care as a mojo bag. The dice (2,3,4, or more) respond based on the numerical outcome of the toss. Recently, there has been renewed interest in divination, known as "casting bones,"; a process in which several animal bones (typically opossum or hen) thrown on the ground or on a fabric cause Vatican harm according to the forms they might take. Although some root physicians are now using it, astrology is banned from the hoodoo tradition since mastering it requires geometric and mathematical understanding that goes beyond the regular training of the conjuremen of the past, who were frequently uneducated. The most unusual methods are the dominoes, which, when mixed face down on the table, chosen at random, and interpreted according to the numbering, give a valid means of divination; another method is the table OUIJA, which usually is used to communicate with the spirits; and finally, the "cup of knowledge," a special tea cup with the inside decorated with symbols (cards or others) that give answers depending on which signs are covered by the residues of tea, coffee, or variou

In this book, we will look closely at the most often used medium: playing cards; eventually, we will provide some fundamental indicators and a conventional interpretation.

Spell or Conjuring

The hoodoo spell is more appropriately known as a begging spell, and its contents are as diverse as you can imagine. It is categorized according to the action desired, and then we discuss asking for blessings, curses, money, love, power, health, and justice. They are often classed according to traditional "color" associations: white for the blessing, black for the curse, green for money, crimson for love, purple for power, blue for health, and brown for justice. Curses of blessing include all exorcisms that seek to drive away bad spirits, purify people or environments, and attract good spirits; curses of curses include actual curses, revenge, expulsion, punishment of evil tongues, and harassing characters; curses of love have to do with "ligaments," attract love, cement the couple, or help them find a new lover; and curses of power seek to make some people submissive. None of these categories are exact and impassable divisions, and new ones are often developed based on the context and the desired activity. Herbs, prayers, powders, oils, bags, stones, dolls, animal remains, and items, among other things, may be used to perform them. Unlike other magical procedures and ideologies, these "tools" do not have a specific shape and are not required.

There are no knives, sticks, or cups dedicated to one symbolism over another; the root doctor frequently works with what he has at the time. Let us recall, in reality, that although the conjure man of the past could not always rely on intricate symbolic solutions or read classic literature, he did have adequate time to dedicate to study and preparation. Everything was given to one's intelligence and traditional wisdom. Things have changed throughout time, but the inherent simplicity of hoodoo has not. Many two-headed physicians may find acceptable remedies in a kitchen furnished with some spice and a piece of cloth, some soil obtained from a certain spot, an oil created by infusion, a candle, and a bible. The conjure man is satisfied to follow the days of the week, occasionally the moon phase, and in some instances, even the clock hands (when both go up the "good" spells, when both go down the "bad" spells). The European magician is outfitted with specially designed clothing and instruments, but the hoodoo practitioner is likely to wear the same clothes he wears to work every day. The magician prepares himself via fasting, penance, and purification, whereas the two-headed doctor is content with a spray of holy water in circumstances when a herbal bath is required. All of this had the benefit of being able to be concealed and naturally indecipherable for anybody who did not know the topic during the period of slavery. In the next chapters, we shall look at various instances of ritual; virtually always, prayers or psalms are chanted throughout the execution; in producing powders, amulets, conducting purifications, and erecting altars, each psalm is connected with achieving a certain result (money, love, victory against the enemy, etc.). I will say which ones when absolutely required; the proper references in the list of psalms and their application may be found in a particular chapter of this work.

The Sacred Space

In the practice of the root doctor, the holy space is a natural rather than sanctified area that takes form in the place and time of the magic operation and ceases to be special at the completion of the operation. The crossroads and the graveyard are sacred locations, but any room or area may become one. Complex consecrations, ceremonial precautions, and symbolic safeguards are not employed for fast activities such as lighting a candle rubbed with different oils or assembling a bag full of amulets. The two-headed doctor is engrossed in the spiritual realm where he lives, and the hoodoo procedure is quick and easy. The spirits recognize him, and he compensates them for their services with sacrifices and prayers. Even in sophisticated operations, "ceremonial rings" or "invocation triangles" are seldom erected in the European style to shield oneself from apparitions of spirits since the spirits are always free and present in these areas. Consider that a handful of cemetery land is said to hold a spirit and that some root physicians have hundreds of jars (depending on the graves they've visited, to employ in various spells).

It was and still is necessary to set off a certain area for performing certain spells. In general, we may talk of "hoodoo chambers," a fact common now but uncommon when the hoodoo was first discovered. In any case, these are chambers where all of the conjure man's preparations, tools, and items are "stored" and where the conjure man conducts his rituals. In these rooms, you may construct other forms of holy places that are not currently accessible, such as the crossroads, by setting a candle in each corner of the area. It is the appropriate location for permanent altars or long-term procedures that take days or even months to complete.

The altar

Whereas in European magic, the altar is a single, dedicated item, in hoodoo, we talk of altars in the plural since the conjure man often possesses more than one. As a result, depending on the approach utilized, the 'activity,' there will be particular altars devoted to more than one purpose, which may be permanent or temporary. Typically, the altar is not sanctified in the literal meaning of the term, and its power is derived only from what is gathered there. The easiest solution is to provide some concrete instances. An altar for love will be dominated by the colors red and pink, with simple red candles shaped like a phallus or vagina, sexual symbols, depictions of genitals, magnetic stones paired and loaded with magnetic powder, depictions of hearts, violets, roots of John, the conqueror, images of saints related to love such as St. Valentine or gods such as Shiva and Parvati depicted in sexual union, oils and dust for love and sex, and so on.

An altar for money and play will be green in color and will include dice, green candles, $ and € symbols, single magnetic stones, coins (especially leap years), alligator or rabbit teeth and legs, chestnut chestnuts, dust, and oils for luck and money, playing cards, horseshoes, depictions of Chinese fortune gods, lottery tickets with special numerical combinations, and so on.

Finally, a cursed altar will be black in appearance, with pepper and chili powder, curse oils, goofer dust, images of the devil, black cats, pins, nails, rag dolls, black candles, bones, graveyard land, portrayals of Baron Samedi and Maman Brigitte, Kali, and so on.

Instead of having a "handyman" altar (which is equally conceivable and, in certain situations, quite useful), it is usually better to undo an altar that is no longer required and redo an altar that is now needed. A "handyman" altar would confound the situation, and maybe even the spirits, and would have to be rather large to accommodate all of the appropriate things.

The materials

The items that are employed in the practice of aversions are nearly limitless. They are divided into four categories: vegetable, animal, mineral, and manufactured items. Among the vegetables are herbs, oils, incense, bones, shells, hair, skins (snake, for example), and teeth; among the animals are minerals, earth, stones, some types of oil, and dust of various kinds; and among the artifacts are candles, amulets, cloths, nails, bags, and everything you need to contain, sprinkle, hold, and so on.

Sometimes they serve more than one purpose, such as the root of John the conqueror, which is used for both good luck at games and for love or to produce oils. Also, excellent work by magic.

Even here, the oils are in the thousands and are often utilized commercially to save the time and waste of producing them alone (which is still doable). They are oils with witty names (van-van, zulazula, like to me, night vision, swift luck, and so on), often mixing more than one essential oil extracted from herbs or simply an infusion of herbs in vegetable oil (almond or olive oil). Sometimes they are mineral oils in which stones are submerged, which should impart a certain power to the oil rather than another. In her book "golden secrets of mystic oils," Anna Riva categorizes over 500 of them and explains how they operate (but not the formula). They are used to activate mojo bags, rub candles, create cleansing baths, scent rooms, or to perfume clothing. To enhance the activity, they are occasionally combined with the grass from which they are derived.

Similarly, incense is often powdered before being placed over lighted charcoals or pressed into geometric patterns to be burned directly. They are used to scent and cleanse the surroundings. Instead, the powders are strewn on clothing, letters, traces, or in front of people's doors and in places where you don't want to go. Sometimes you may discover a renowned formula's oil, incense, and powder, all of which serve the same goal and support each other.

Another issue is candles, whose color is more essential than their aroma and which have their own position in hoodoo practice. In the 1940s, Henry Gamache, the first to create an exact table of correspondence between the colors of candles and deeds to be done, devoted a whole treatise ("master book of burning candles"), reading which you can see how much affected current magic practice.

The candles are employed not just by lighting them but also by doing so at specified times, on unique altars, and even by making them "migrate" from one configuration to another day by day. They may, however, be "loaded" by rubbing them with oil and rolling them in pre-prepared herbs. There are numerous types of candles, ranging from those that are simply colored to those that have evocative shapes (crucifixes, phallic symbols, devils, embraced lovers) to those that are enclosed in glass and have the image of the saint incorporated and are guaranteed to burn for more than a month.

Animal remains are also popular in the practice of hoodoo. Powders, amulets, mojo hands, spells, and spells of all types are made from teeth and snake skins, snail shells, shells, urine, menstrual blood, hair, and dried spiders. The "cat eyes" (really a colorful section of a tropical shell), alligator legs and fangs, rattles of the same-named

snake, and lastly, the raccoon penile bone (yep, the raccoon has a bone in the penis and is used as an amulet of
love) are among the most unusual.

Finally, there are the artifacts: coffin nails, phallic amulets, horseshoes, tiny nuts, nails, pins, fetishes, saint figures, bags, textiles, food paper, and different amulets.

CHAPTER 2

Hoodoo Magic Spells

Voodoo is a religious practice. Hoodoo is the darkness that lies at the foot of Voodoo. Voodoo is an African religious group that practices magic rituals. It has a group of gods called the Loah, as well as rites, hierarchies, symbols of power, temples, and initiations.

Hoodoo does not include any of these. It is a series of magical rituals that seldom has a clearly defined theological meaning; rather, it might draw from a variety of cults, including Voodoo.

The core of Hoodoo is the pursuit of worldly benefits via sorcery.

The end justifies the means in Hoodoo. Because the rituals have a personal stamp, there are no collective ceremonies. The practitioner works alone, and his contact with the spirits is close and personal unless he wishes to teach his knowledge or the ritual necessitates the participation of others.

Hoodoo originated in Africa and mainly expanded in America, notably in the New Orleans region. Marie Laveau is perhaps its most renowned practitioner.

This kind of magic originated in Africa, but it gained popularity in America following the slave trade, approximately 1600 AD. Conjure men or Root Doctors are the practitioners' names.

The Bible is the most often utilized literature, and the Psalms, in particular, are frequently used to reinforce a spell. This is because of the heinous force in these ancient prayers, which have been repeated for millennia, endowing them with extraordinary magical power. The Sixth and Seventh Books of Moses are valid, as are two grimoires from the Renaissance era, particularly for seals.

In contrast to the Western magician, the Conjure Man can easily execute his rituals with a kitchen stocked with spices, a piece of cloth, a smidgeon of earth, some infusion oil, some candles, and a Bible.

Hoodoo practitioners use plants, prayers, powders, bags, stones, cloth dolls, animal carcasses, and diverse things.

The substances are often interchangeable, and the practitioner determines the amounts and quantities. The same oils, potions, and substances may differ depending on their origins and traditions.

White Magic
Simple Money Attraction Spell

The following items are required for the Magic Ritual:

- A green candle

- A pointed tool to engrave the candle

- A bowl

- Water

- Seven-star anise seeds

The Ritual of Magic:
Engrave the following text on the green candle using the pointed object:

Chrimata. Dirua. Maritupe.

Fill the basin with water and ignite the green candle.

Pour in one-star anise seed at a time, repeating the following magic formula for each seed:

Sau ia ia te au chrimata. Sau ia ia te au dirua. Sau ia ia te au

maritupe. By the virtue of this seed, I will prosper. Para chrimata.

Para dirua. Para maritupe. A little richer I shall be. Yes, I do. Yes, I

will be a little richer.

Allow the candle to burn out.

Allow the seeds to soak in the water for seven days before collecting them and storing them in your wallet eternally.

To win the game, do the Saint Lucia ritual.
The Magic Ritual requires the following items:

- seawater,

- a green silk ribbon,

- a fresh terracotta vase, and

- seven white candles.

The Ritual of Magic:

Fill the new clay vase halfway with seawater.

Place the seven white candles around the terracotta vase,
then light them one at a time, saying:

*O wonderful Saint Lucia, who has your name in
the light, hear me.*

Wash the green silk ribbon inside the terracotta vase with
the sea water, reciting the creed three times:

*I believe in God, Almighty Father, Creator of heaven
and earth. And*

*in Jesus Christ, His only Son, our Lord, who was
conceived of the*

*Holy Spirit was born of the Virgin Mary, suffered
under Pontius*

*Pilate, was crucified, died and was buried; he
descended into hell;*

*on the third day he rose from the dead; he ascended
to heaven, he*

*sits at the right hand of God the Father Almighty:
from there he will*

come to judge the living and the dead. I believe in the Holy Spirit, the

Holy Catholic Church, the communion of saints, the remission of

sins, the resurrection of the flesh, eternal life. Amen.

Allow the candles to burn and the green silk ribbon to dry in the sun.

Take the green silk ribbon as an amulet for good luck in the game.

Brazilian magic to boost your own strength

The following items are required for the Magic Ritual:

- A white candle

- A glass of coconut milk

- Two teaspoons of saffron

- A fresh sponge

The Ritual of Magic:

Light the white candle and, without blinking, repeat the following magic formula as long as you can keep your eyes open:

Prepare a hot bath while the candle burns. Pour in a glass of coconut milk and two teaspoons of saffron. Then soak in the water for a few minutes before repeating the magic recipe with a fresh sponge.

Spell for good fortune
The following items are required for the Magic Ritual:

- A garlic clove

- Parsley

- Halls

- ashes from incense

- A little white silk bag

The Ritual of Magic:
Place the garlic clove, parsley, salt, and incense ashes in the white silk bag. Then visit seven churches and dunk the bag into each of their soups.

After dipping the bag, sit down and pray:

Our Father, who art in heaven, hallowed be thy name, thy kingdom come, thy will be done, on earth as it is in heaven, give us this day our daily bread,

lead us not into temptation, and deliver us from
our enemies who want us evil, and deliver me from
my enemies who want me evil, and deliver me from
my enemies who want me evil. Amen.

Keep the little bag with you always as an amulet to bring you good luck.

Simple Spell To Find Serenity Again
The following items are required for the Magic Ritual:

• twelve white candles.

The Magic Ritual:
On a full moon night, you form a circle of white candles around yourself.

Light the candles one by one, reciting this prayer with each lit candle:

Sub tuum praesidium confugimus, sancta Dei Gen-
etrix, nostras

deprecationes ne despicias in necessitatibus, sed a
periculis cunctis

libera nos semper, Virgo gloriosa et benedicta. Amen.

Maintain your position inside the circle of candles, which emits a bright light that envelops you and frees you from any evil thoughts.

The Happiness Potion

Required for the Magic Ritual:

- A little ampoule with the cap

- A dried and crushed "dandelion" (dandelion blossom)

- 1 tablespoon dried oregano

- 1 tablespoon cinnamon powder

- 1 tablespoon dried thyme powder

- a total of seven pine needles

The Ritual of Magic:

Close the bottle after adding all of the powdered herbs.

Kneel to the east and recite Psalm 7 seven times:

> *Lord, my God, in you I have found refuge: save me from those who persecute me and set me free, so that you do not rip me apart like a lion, tearing me apart without anybody liberating me. Lord, my God, if I have behaved in this manner, if I have*

done unjustly, if I have returned a friend with evil, if I have stripped my foes for no cause, let the enemy chase and join me, crush my life on the ground, and throw my honor into dust. Arise, O Lord, in your fury, against the rage of my enemies, be unshaken, my God, make a decision! The gathering of people envelops you: return from above to conquer it! The Lord is the one who judges the nations. Judge me, Lord, according to my justice and innocence. Stop the wicked's evil. You who examine the mind and heart, O just God, strengthen the virtuous. My protection is in God, who rescues the virtuous. God is a just judge who gets offended every day. Does he not return to polish his sword, care for his sheep, and aim his bow? He sharpens his arrows and prepares his implements for destruction. Behold, the evil one conceives injustice, bears wickedness, and bears falsehoods. He digs a deep hole and falls into the abyss he has dug; his wickedness and violence fall on his head. I will praise the Lord for his righteousness and sing the Most High's name.

Keep the ampoule with you at all times as an amulet for good luck.

The Vase Of Prosperity
Needed for the Magic Ritual:

- A terracotta jar

- Three green candles

- Three golden candles

- Seven leaves of rosemary

- Seven bay leaves

- Seven basil leaves

- Seven leaves of thyme

- Seven lavender leaves

- Seven Cloves

- Oil

- Three silver coins

- A wooden stick

The Magic Ritual:

Place all of the herbs in the clay jar with the three silver coins, then cover with oil.

Arrange the three green candles and three golden candles around the jar in the following order: one green, one golden, one green, one golden, and so on.

Turn on the candles.

Mix the contents of the jar clockwise with the wooden stick, repeating the magic phrase seven times:

Paisa. Panam. Pecunia. Penz. Para. Dirua.

Then, recite this magical phrase seven times while mixing the contents of the jar counterclockwise:

Aurid. Arap. Znep. Manap. Asiap.

Break the wooden stick in half and place it in the jar. Allow the candles to burn out and keep the jar at a location in your home near a door or window forever.

Simple And Effective Spell To Free a Person From The Evil Eye

Needed for the Magic Ritual:

- A mirror of garlic

- Halls

- Oil

- Water

- A copper pot

- Three white candles

- A photograph of the person you want to free from the evil eye.

The Magic Ritual:

Place three white candles around the copper pot and ignite them one at a time while saying the Glory:

Glory to the Father, Son, and Holy Spirit. As it was in the beginning, as it is now and always will be, forever and ever. Amen.

Fill the copper saucepan halfway with water.

Apply the garlic on a picture of the person you wish to protect from the evil eye.

Chop the garlic and add it to the saucepan with a little salt and oil.

Then, while repeating this magical phrase, burn the photograph:

> *Garlic, salt and oil. Go away evil eye that I don't want you. Burn the*

evil eye. Broken is the enchantment. In the name of the Father, the

Son and the Holy Spirit.

Add some salt and olive oil to the saucepan once more.

Throw the water from the pot into a brook the following morning while chanting three Our Fathers and three Hail Marys.

Prevention To Protect Yourself
Needed for the Magic Ritual:

• None

The Magic Ritual:

Go to a field at dawn and repeat this prayer three times:

Pater noster dei sanctorum. Maria bella angelorum. Beautiful Mary

sleeping. And the baby Jesus appeared to her in a dream. Dear, I

dreamt that at the ordeal they brought you. Golden crowns have lifted you up and thorns have planted you. What you are saying is

truth, the Christ answered to your mother. And whoever says this

three times in a field, is not afraid of water, thunder and lightning.

Ancient Spell To Attract Money
Needed for the Magic Ritual:

- A white candle

- A fresh chestnut leaf

- A silver coin

The Magic Ritual:

Light the white candle on a Monday night with the new moon and chant five Our Fathers and five Hail Marys. Wrap the silver coin in the chestnut leaf and recite the following magic formula 10 times:

Today is the moon, tomorrow is Mars. My fate, my beautiful one don't

leave me alone. Come meet me, do not frighten me, let me discover

the wealth.

Allow the candle to burn out while keeping the silver coin wrapped in chestnut leaf in your wallet.

Red Magic
Spell To Be Thought Intensely By a Person

Needed for the Magic Ritual:

- A new mirror

- Your photograph

- A photograph of the other person

- Adhesive tape

- A white candle

The Magic Ritual:

Place the picture of the person you want to think about you in front of the mirror, with the image facing the reflecting surface and your photograph on the back. Tie the two images together with adhesive tape and arrange them on the mirror so they don't fall off.

Turn on the white candle.

Recite the following magic formula 49 times while holding the mirror at your heart:

Every time you see your reflection you will think of me. Thame.

Skefteis.

Let the candle wear out and keep the mirror under your bed indefinitely.

Potion To Attract Love, Friendship & Luck
Items required for the Magical Ritual:

- Rose Water;

- Three Strawberries;

- Three Vanilla Pods;

- Three Tablespoons each of Cocoa and Salt;

- One Pan;

- One Glass Bottle.

- a piece of paper,

- a red marker

The Mystical Ceremony:
Toss everything into a saucepan and bring it to a simmer for half an hour.

Put the following enchantment into writing using the red pen:

Pure love. Strong love. Open all the doors to me.
Pure love. Strong

friendship. Luck be favorable to me.

Toss the rolled-up piece of paper into the transparent container. Then, using the filter, transfer the liquid from the saucepan to the bottle, and seal it.

Shake the bottle seven times while reciting the spell you typed on the label.

The bottle should be stored in the dark forever.

Easy And Effective Love Spell With Hair
Items required for the Magical Ritual:

- Five strands of the desired lover's hair,

- five of your own hair,

- a red woolen thread,

- a red candle, a green candle, and

- a yellow candle.

The Mystical Ceremony:

Arrange the candles in a triangle on the floor.

Put the five hairs of the person you wish to fall in love with you in the center of the three candles and bind them together with the red woollen thread.

Each time you light a candle, beginning with the red one (and continuing with the green and yellow ones), say this magical formula:

Ure, sanctus spiritus, renes nostros et cor nostrum, domine.

Burn the candles down to nothing and bury the bundle of hair close to where the target resides to make them fall in love with you.

Powerful Ritual To Make Falling In Love
Items required for the Magical Ritual:

- Halls

- A lock of hair of the person you want to fall in love with

- Nine red candles

- Nine green candles

- Nine yellow candles

The Magic Ritual:

Draw a huge circle on the floor with salt and line its perimeter with all the candles, switching their colors as you go (one red, one green, one yellow, one red, one green, one yellow, etc.).

Step within the circle and, beginning with the candle facing east, light each candle in clockwise order around the circle.

Put a lock of the person you wish to fall in love with in your right hand, shut your eyes, and mentally call out their name 99 times.

Don't bother replacing the candles, and leave the hair in your pillowcase as long as you want.

Ishtar's Love Ligament
This Magical Ritual Requires:

- One meter of crimson silk ribbon

The Magic Ritual:

For 48 nights in a row, while tying a knot in our silk knot and repeating the following magic formula,

In the name of Ishtar, the one who makes everything fruitful, I tie you to me, and your love for me day by day as ivy on the wall will grow. So be it. So it will be.

At first light on the 49th day, take the ashes of the ribbon you burned and disperse them at a rural intersection.

Love ligament of Venus with apple
Needed for the Magic Ritual:

- A healthy apple

- Two squares of paper

- A hair of the person you want to make fall in love

- Your hair

- Needle and red thread

- A wooden box

- Bay leaves

The Magic Ritual:

A little piece of paper is stained with blood, and on one side you write your name and the target's.

After slicing the apple in half and scooping out the seeds, you may insert the squares and the two hairs were knotted together with a piece of paper.

Sew the two halves of the apple together with red thread so they won't come apart.

Wrap the apple with bay leaves and place it in the wooden box.

Put the red candle on top of the box before closing it.

After you've lit the light, repeat this enchantment seven times:

> *Venus mother, immortal Venus, daughter of Jupiter.*
> *To you who*
>
> *alone dominate nature and without you nothing is*
> *born. I invoke you*
>
> *and I beg you. Let (name) quickly come to me.*
> *Make him fall madly*
>
> *in love with me. That he can no longer eat, drink*
> *or sleep except with*
>
> *me. O Venus, glorious goddess, to you whom I said*
> *"if he does not*
>
> *love you already, he will soon do so" I address my*
> *humble begging.*
>
> *Make him fall in love with me, even against his*
> *will! So be it and so it*

Put the candle out and the box beneath your bed. indefinitely.

Wine Ritual To Bring Back The Lover
Needed for the Magic Ritual:

- A glass jar

- Red wine

- A red candle

- Seven sheets of red paper

- A black felt-tip pen

- Scissors

The Magic Ritual:

Using scissors, cut out all seven sheets of paper so that they form seven little hearts and write these words on each one:

(name of the loved one you want to bring back)
cinta saya kembali

kepada saya.

Light the red candle and recite this magic formula seven times:

Kerana scheva mencintai saya lagi. Kembali kepada saya. Cinta

saya lagi dan lagi.

Fill the jar with red wine.

Place one small heart at a time on the candle flame and while it is burning throw it into the jar saying:

Kembali kepada saya.

After burning all the little paper hearts close the glass jar hermetically and let the candle consume itself.

Keep the jar under your bed indefinitely.

Black Magic
Macumbero

Needed for the Magic Ritual:

- A black envelope

- Cemetery land

- A photograph of the person to curse

- Eleven old and rusty nails

- A black candle

The Magic Ritual:

One Friday evening, during a waning moon, insert in the black envelope the photograph of the person you want to curse together with the cemetery land and the eleven old and rusty nails. Then seal the envelope and go to a country crossing.

Just after midnight bury the envelope in the incronym and light the black candle.

Hold the black candle in your left hand and recite this magic formula eleven times:

Adja gbe o. Kutu adja gbe o.

After reciting the formula, blow out the candle by sticking it upside down in the place where you buried the envelope. Then go home without looking back.

Dust to cause discord
Needed for the Magic Ritual:

- Nine dried nettle leaves

- A whole dried chilli pepper

- Cemetery land

- A mortar

The Magic Ritual:

The following magical phrase must be spoken nineteen times while pounding nettle leaves, chili pepper, and cemetery dirt in a mortar:

Pore bael pore. Separates. Divide. Tear. Tear. And one runs away from the other.

The "cursed dust" should be sprinkled at their normal meeting spot.

Brazilian Spell For a Man To Reject His Wife
Needed for the Magic Ritual:

- A handkerchief impregnated with the seed of the desired man

- A glass bottle with a stopper

- White rum

The Magic Ritual:

Place the handkerchief inside the glass container, on which is impregnated the seed of the selected male, and screw on the lid.

It would be best to bury the bottle upside down somewhere close to the man's house or a cemetery.

White rum should be poured in the shape of a cross around the spot where the bottle was buried, and then you should depart without looking back.

Curse Tarragon
Needed for the Magic Ritual:

- A potato

- Nine pins

- Nine black candles

- A piece of red fabric

- Nine dried nettle leaves

- Olive oil

The Magic Ritual:

Place the nine black candles around the potato and light them one by one reciting this magic formula:

> *For Tarragon I invoke you, for Tarragon I wake you, hellish spirits, I*
>
> *beg you, make my drawing.*

Stick one pin at a time in the potato, intensely visualizing the image of the person you want to curse and recite these words for each pin:

For Tarragon that (name of the person you want to curse) be cursed!

Grease your left hand's fingers and draw a cross three times on the potato bundle as you wrap it in the black fabric.

The potato should be buried in the vicinity of a graveyard.

Curse of fire
Needed for the Magic Ritual:

• A tuft of hair of the person you want to curse

• Wax

• A black candle

The Magic Ritual:

Use wax to mould a figurine and insert the tuft of hair of the person you want to curse into it.

Light the black candle and recite this magic formula:

Spirits of the shadow, allow me to exercise your power against

(name of the person you want to curse).

Slowly burn the wax figurine with the flame of the candle and recite this magic formula nine times:

It is not the wax that I am burning, but the body and soul of (name of

the person you want to curse). May the fire consume you. May you

be cursed. With all my poison. With all my poison. With all my

poison.

Once the figurine has dissolved, collect the wax residues and bury them near a cemetery.

Spell to subdue a man
Needed for the Magic Ritual:

• Seven red candles

• Jasmine incense

• A photograph of the man you want to submit to you

The Magic Ritual:

Strip down completely.

Arrange the seven red candles in a circle and light them one by one reciting this magic formula:

> *In the name of Aletto, Megera and Tisiphon. Let my will be done. Let*
>
> *your will be done. For a soul and a body. For a body and a soul. Let*
>
> *my will be done. Let your will be done.*

Light the jasmine incense and hold the photograph of the man and recite these magic words thirty times:

> *For Aletto, you obey me. By Megera, you perish to me. By Tisyphon,*
>
> *you obey me.*

Every time you repeat the magic words try to increase the intensity of your voice and intensely visualize the image of the man in question completely submitted to you.

Let the candles wear out and keep the photograph under your bed indefinitely.

Red Apple Curse
Needed for the Magic Ritual:

- A red apple

- A tuft of hair of the person to curse

- Eleven old and rusty nails

- Eleven black candles

The Magic Ritual:

Make a hole in the apple (without cutting it) and insert the person's tuft of hair to curse into it.

Then, while chanting the following magic formula, you should light a black candle, heat a nail in the flame, and insert the nail into an apple.

I curse your flesh with fire. I curse your soul with iron.

With the other 10 candles and nails, carry out the procedure once again.

Put the red apple in a hole in the ground near the front door of the person you want to curse.

CHAPTER 3

The Hoodoo Congregation

The New York Congregation is made up of several smaller congregations, all of which share a temporary community on Hart Island.

Hart Island is a small piece of deserted land in the Bronx that is home to the remains of over a million individuals, although few New Yorkers are aware of its existence. Since 1869, the city's homeless and underprivileged have been buried on this half-square-kilometer of ground, viewable from a corner of the Bronx.

Several empty buildings on the island were once a mental hospital, a TB sanatorium, and a place where young people were locked up. There is still no marker indicating the names of the deceased. This is how it seems to a no-mag reader, even if the truth is different. Many obstructions on the island make it impossible for No-Mag to have a good look around. Hart Island's history is full of failed projects that would have made it the center of reclamation efforts, military outposts, and other things it never did. Because of these same rules, the no-mag "guests" of the island can only stay in one place, where they have to spend their short, uncomfortable stays. Outside, hoodoo and voodoo-made trinkets, amulets, and protections are sold from houses and caravans that are hidden from view by spells. Sounds of rituals being done within the grounds of the coven, where their powers are greater than ever and fuelled by the spirits that inhabit the site, can be heard reverberating through the air. At the intersections of the winding paths that connect the small lanes, you can see altars with images and idols from many different religions. The Mojo Moco is the primary gateway into the Congrega area. It may be found on City Island, just across from the cemetery and beside Barrons Boatyard. These waters protect the boats and are also the route used by the Fantom Bato, a magical ferry that takes passengers to Hart Island. Members of the Cabal use different obstacles and rituals to keep people from getting on the island and into the shop.

- That's a no-mag barrier, man. The unease the no-mags
  sense grows the closer they come to the place. At first,

it was simply in their heads, like they were being watched or there was an oppressive presence around. The closer you go, the more physically uncomfortable you feel; heart attack symptoms include dizziness, rapid heartbeat, nausea, and lightheadedness.

- Protection against vampires In light of the current vampire troubles, hoodoo, and voodoo wizards have erected several barricades around coven places. Vampires cannot enter a house to which they have not been invited. Thus, these fundamental obstacles make use of this fact.

- Barrier against enmity. Those who go into a church to hurt its members feel an immediate and inversely proportional weakening of their own physical and mental resources. This implies that individuals who want to do things like completely wipe off the congregation's population may suffer a fatal heart attack just attempting to enter their lands.

- The majority of congregants, however, experience only mild symptoms, including a temporary reduction in physical and magical power, dizziness, and, in extreme circumstances, fainting. The barrier's effects may be felt as early as Fantom Bato Harbor and intensify as one draws closer to the center of Hart Island. In addition, they may be found at Mojo Moco.

- Arms-free zone. Bringing weapons into the Cabal is permitted, although leaving them at the Fantom Bato Port shops is advised. It's because any weapon becomes more ineffective as one nears the center of Hart Island. Progressive beveling of blades, rust that makes metals weaker, and, in the case of automatic weapons, loosening of gears and parts that hold them together, which quickly jams the mechanisms, belts, and non-metal parts that are prone to rust and start to wear out early. Both local voodoo and hoodoo practitioners and tourists should leave their weapons at home.

- Protects from materialization. Within Cabal territory, entrances to portals and teleports to other locations and universes are sealed.

- The alarm system. Let's say a taboo has been disregarded. Then, a sudden wonderful wind will blow up on Hart Island, resonating only the glass and metal attached to such barriers from the porches. To tell the difference between a steady breeze and a breached barrier, many nearby homes install a trinket that is attached to the barriers and another that is not.

Root Doctors

Hoodoo magicians have naturally built a network of covens over time so that people interested in the practice can share and get information about it. Hoodoo covens have a specific name, but they are always made up of a shifting membership, including long-term residents of a certain area and individuals still on the move around the United States. Given that, it's no longer necessary to have an official Hoodoo school, as anybody may pass on what they've learned. Still, those who stand out for the amount of information they can impart are known as root doctors or two-headed doctors.

They are addressed with the virtual honorific titles of mother, father, uncle, aunt, and doctor (doctor). A person may become a Hoodoo Doctor simply by solving difficulties and demonstrating time and time again that they have something that can serve in the present scenario, earning the respect of the community (a group of individuals who do not practice hoodoo) or the coven. Root doctors in many parts of the South, including Louisiana (particularly around New Orleans), Alabama (near Mobile), and Mississippi (an area adjacent to the river of the same name), are generally held in high regard, both by less experienced hoodoo wizards and by those who are unfamiliar with hoodoo magic but nonetheless come into contact with them.

The New York congregation put a lot of faith in Papa Chinue, even though they had yet to plan on a leader being there. Aside from overseeing the congregation's business in general, he was also in charge of its relationships with other local groups. Since he departed New York in March 2018, the hoodoo magicians have followed the ancient customs, restarting the practice of magic and controlling the coven connections without any person who might constitute a legitimate leader.

The Congregation Of Santa Muerte

It's more accurately called a coven, or a collection of individuals gathered for religious purposes, than a sect, but the two terms are not mutually exclusive. The Godmother is the spiritual leader of the coven, and she performs hoodoo ceremonies in order to get Santa Muerte's blessing and cure the ill or at least ease their suffering. She may also conduct Santa Muerte's curses and levy bills upon the wicked.

The worship of Santa Muerte is not meant to replace Christianity. Instead, it is a celebration of death as a natural part of life that even Jesus couldn't avoid but which he eventually accepted as a step on the way to God. Some people need clarification on a straightforward explanation for where this dedication comes from. The Catholic missionaries to Mexico brought Christianity to what was likely a pre-Columbian cult dedicated to a god. As a result, the members of this coven honor Santa Muerte.

The practice of piety towards Santa Muerte is often seen unfavorably in the media. The media gladly portrays it as having ties to criminal activity and drug trafficking. In recent years, the Mexican government has told the army to destroy a lot of altars, often by saying they were built illegally. This is seen as a symbolic move against narcos and a way to make the Catholic Church happy, which is in trouble in Latin America, where evangelical churches are growing. Because of this, most cult members in North America have fled to the Bronx, a relatively safe neighborhood in New York City. They became a part of the ideas and rituals of the local coven, but they were still welcomed as full members.

Aside from being the "saint of the narcos," the drug lords who control large swaths of Mexico, the Nia Blanca (another name for the Santa Muerte, called the white woman because of the color of her bones) is the patron saint of the poor, the abandoned, the last, and anyone who feels precarious and insecure in society, including prisoners, vendors, housewives, cleaning women, and the unemployed. After all, precariousness is a subjective notion, or rather, given the fragility of the human situation, it is universal. This coven makes no exception to the welfare state in admitting its acolytes.

It should be made clear that the Nia is in no way a figure who is requested for the death of someone; rather, the Nia is asked for protection, a favor, mediation, or the return of a loved one (or in conjunction with him, if he has fled), something one would be embarrassed to ask of an official Catholic saint. Since it affects everyone equally, death is therefore equated with perfect justice. Death itself, personified and holy, has the capacity to prevent or delay your own personal death or to let you pass on swiftly, painlessly, and without fear, if the time has come. People show respect for Santa Muerte by keeping altars in their homes and getting together regularly to pray.

Santa Muerte shrines. Since the Our Lady of the Holy Death cult has been formally rejected by the Catholic Church, her adherents (mostly Catholics) maintain secret altars in the home and worship secretly before the Blessed Sacrament. It is common practice to display pictures of the diosa on Santa Muerte altars. Holy Death figures dressed in "black," "red," "green," "white," "yellow," and "golden" are all common representations. It may also be gray, blue-celeste, or even purple at times. The classical depiction of Diana has her holding scales, a scythe, and even a globe; the esoteric depiction includes an hourglass and a puppet to symbolize her foreboding position in the tally of human life. Lighted candles and various donations, including expensive jewelry, cash, fruits, sweets, cigarettes, and beer, have been left around the "Saint's" shrine.

The risks associated with religious devotion. The common Mexican opinion is that superficially and momentarily invoking or voting for her without a good cause is hazardous. Some believe that the penalty for such a deed and a broken pledge would be the loss of a loved one rather than one's own life. Santa Muerte has a reputation for being quite envious.

The black congregation

Hart Island is protected by MACUSA because it is a neutral territory. For this reason, practitioners of voodoo and hoodoo cannot just open their homes to criminals and black magicians as any other citizen would. Members of the Cabal who have mastered a kind of magic that, due to the ancient history of sacrifices and the like, risks degenerating into lawlessness if not correctly adhered to, are eager to obey these regulations even more rigidly.

The congregation's magicians hid in a complex network of tunnels after the signing of the Statute of Secrecy in 1692; these tunnels eventually merged with the city's sewage system. Most people today think this sunken city is made up, and even if it did exist, as suggested by the few clues we have from a long time ago, it is thought to have been shut down and abandoned a long time ago. The submerged metropolis is really much more genuine. Hoodoo and voodoo practitioners live in the shadows. They are firmly rooted in their ancient traditions and, because they don't judge, they think it's okay to sacrifice animals and even people. The Court of Miracles is where lawbreakers go to hide from the rest of the congregation. Even within the congregation, only a minority is aware of the existence of the Miracle Court. The port is accessible from the open sea side of the Fantom Bato mooring. An underground passageway formed by a gap in a row of tombstones. This region is secure thanks to the same barriers that keep the rest of Hart Island safe, but the Court of Miracles has additional safeguards that even the Cabal's wizards can't breach. The Ancients warn against venturing into this cursed region. Superstition thrives when people are afraid to approach something out of ignorance for fear of what could lie within. Getting to the heart of the court from the beginning tunnels is daunting due to the darkness and lack of landmarks. Each home had a distinct doorway leading into the tunnels since they were excavated into the stone walls. There is a great deal of harmony inside the Black Cabal, and it is not unusual for members to trade favors and spells with one another. Actually, the doors are a point of exchange: when a magician needs a spell, a ritual, or a component, he knocks on the door, and the residents of the house provide to open it after hearing the secret word of their exercise, which is different for each household and is chosen by the residents themselves. Words are the foundation of the sort of magic that bonds the Black Cabal together and gives its members their magical abilities.

Although the Black Cabal lacks a true leader in the traditional sense, it does have a spokesperson in Logos. He is the go-to guy when there's trouble on the home front; he's in charge of maintaining the secrecy and security of the Black Congregation, and he controls the most vital parts of daily life there. His most important "events" are based on the idea that the Black Congregation needs to be open and united in order to stay alive. In the event of a revelation, the truth must be fully exposed and discussed; everyone has a voice and a right to be heard. All Black Congregation rituals begin and end with this:

THE INQUISITION

When an internal dispute is finally resolved, that is the Inquisition. If there is discord between many factions, everyone meets at the Great Square, where a box is permanently kept. The disputants take turns exposing their side of the narrative to Logos and the audience, who are free to clap, jeer, or otherwise voice their approval or disapproval. For this reason, the ceremony will continue until everyone who wishes to speak has done so. After a first round of debating, during which both sides must wear wreaths of truth-promoting herbs, Logos will come up with a phrase to describe each side's perspective; this word will serve as the parties' names throughout the Inquisition. The next stage will include public statements from each camp in response to what he has said. If there is one, the new name will then be made clear. Logos will get the word if it still needs to be altered. At the end of the Inquisition, he will deliver a final harangue in which he may choose to advocate for one side or the other based on public opinion, change the subject if he has strayed from his original mission, or even encourage a rematch between the opposing parties. The Inquisition is over when each party has a name that distinguishes them not as victims or executioners but as creatures that will end the war or live together.

By posting in this thread, anybody may request to hold an inquisition.

THE PROCESS

Acceptance into the Black Congregation is a ritualized procedure. In contrast to the congregation, where a person may join even if the rest of the community does not fully accept them, there must be a high degree of cohesiveness in the Black Congregation. This is why the Process has concluded, during which the new member stands chained on the stage alone (or with other potential members and Logos), as if about to leave life or death. At first, Logos will begin acting out a portion of his life or whatever he has discovered about himself, whether told by the new member or discovered through other means, given that he is in contact with hoodoo and voodoo wizards of the various American covens, so through them he can have access to a great deal of information, as well as through contact with the Ancestors. The Black Congregation has the right to pass judgment after all the facts are known, and the person's life narrative has been conveyed in expressive language. Everybody has a chance to opine and applaud until the moment of truth: is this outsider one of us? The story is meant to keep people interested and get them to accept the new member of the group fully. Actually, if you want to welcome the new member and answer "yes," you have to stomp your feet when the question is presented. When the newcomer's footsteps reach a certain decibel level, they are welcomed into the coven. If the new member is claimed within two days, their memories from that period are kept, and they are left to fend for themselves on City Island or the Bronx.

Magical Practices

Those who seek Santa Muerte's (Pale Woman) blessing via hoodoo magic will find that their rituals are similar to those utilized by other practitioners, with one key difference. This is incorporating a fourth element into rituals and spells, death, which is now seen as more than just the last stage of life. Santa Muerte devotees see death as the ultimate apogee and rebirth, believing that this is the only way to treat one's own mortality with respect. To reach this goal, you have to be "familiar" with death all your life, looking for the meaning of life without ignoring death and the other way around. This is because both life and death gain significance as a result of living. The magician must, therefore, actively usurp this reality. For the essence of a living creature to be in the spell, it must be killed. This includes plants, which must be burned or destroyed by magic, animals, and people. The more important the creature's death is in the circle of life, the more energy Nia Blanca will give to the spell. The creature's spirit will soar to join the universe's energy, which Catholics see as heaven. In fact, when charms are made in the name of Santa Muerte, the diosa gives her blessing, which is her spiritual force. This force is filled with all the deaths that have happened on earth, so it is almost impossible to use up as long as death is still around. This implies that magic done in her name has even more force than before. The Pale Woman will only bless spells that deal with life and death—protection, healing, and death as bad luck meant to give the unlucky so much bad luck that bad things happen that, in the worst case, could kill them.

Prayer of consecration to Santa Muerte:

Oh!... Santísima Muerte!!

Yo te Suplico Encarecidamente

Que así, Como te formó Dios, inmortal,

With you Gran Poder, sobre Todos los mortales...

Hasta ponerlos, en la Esfera Celeste,

from whence Gozaremos, of a Glorious Day, since Noche...

Para, toda la Eternidad ...

En el Nombre del Padre, del Hijo y del Espíritu Santo...

Yo te Ruego y te Suplico, que te Dignes de ser mi

Protectora…

Desde Ahora;

Y, me Concedas… Todos los Favores, que Yo te Pida:

Hasta el último Día,

Hora y Momento, en que Su, Divina Majestad,

Ordene llevarme, ante Tu presencia."

Oath sanctioned to the consecration:

I will worship Death with total respect.

I will not pronounce his name in vain.

I will adore her in the days I dedicate myself to her.

I will honor all my brothers in religion.

I will not hurt anyone who does not deserve it
according to the will of

the Godhead.

I will not commit any act that may prejudice our
religion that worships

Death.

I will not abuse my spiritual knowledge.

I will not make false testimonies that concern you.

I will not have thoughts that make me profit thanks to you.

CHAPTER 4

Spirits Of Conjure

Many other names have been given to me through-out my life because of my spiritual outlook. I've called myself a Wiccan, a Pagan, a Root Worker, a Two-Headed Doctor, and a host of other names throughout the years. A few of the most often-asked questions I get are:

- What do you believe to be true?

- To whom do you pay homage?

The God I worshiped as a kid was an elderly guy in heaven with white hair and a long white beard who knew everything and saw everything. He blessed the unmarried mother who gave birth to Jesus, his "only-born son," and the eternal God. I learned that he only loved us if we respected his authority and shook when he was around.

When I encountered Wicca, after a spiritual search that led me away from Christianity, I learned that our "God" was really our Mother and Father. The Goddess gives birth to the God, and he grows up and falls in love with her, gets her pregnant, dies, and is reborn at the end of each season. We have not worshiped them as much as we have honored them, and we have always had the freedom to be fully accountable for our own decisions.

The more I learned about Southern folk magic, Hoodoo, and the Gospel, the more he returned to my mind's eye, and the more I realized I had to reevaluate my first impressions of him. To me, Jesus is the epitome of what it means for a human being to have a meaningful connection with God, in contrast to how some magicians consider him a genius or a mythical person.

One of my friends just reminded me that no matter how spiritual you are, others will always doubt your faith. When I discovered that someone close to me thought I worshipped the devil, I was taken aback. It would seem that many individuals still want to know,

- What do you believe in?

- who do you bow down to?

That concludes my response.

"What we have traditionally termed God and shall here refer to as the Spirit is asexual, androgynous, and the purest form of love. To better comprehend the Spirit, many cultures have associated it with various archetypes, such as male, female, and even animal forms (as was the case in ancient Egyptian and Native American belief systems), since humans have trouble relating to something that is all three at once.

A woman who has been mistreated by men may find solace in a heavenly entity that takes the form of a warrior goddess, while a homosexual man who seeks God may see him as a handsome male figure who loves and embraces him.

Some people need help accepting the Spirit's message of forgiveness and unconditional love. So, instead of taking responsibility for their mistakes, people have often pictured their idea of God as having traits that they don't like in themselves. This has led to legends about God being jealous, petty, harsh, loving, kind, and generous. Those who have never had genuine love or companionship may need to see "God" as Satan in order to cope with their suffering, stop blaming "God" for their circumstances, or accept their place in society.

All forms of life, from people to plants to animals to the "lowest" forms of life, have a divine spark, or part of themselves that is the Spirit, that is related to all other life and seeks to merge with the source of this light (cosmic awareness).

Through the holy spark that is present in every life, the Spirit knows what it is like to be alive. Humans may have any and all emotions, sensations, and states of being that other sentient beings share with the Spirit. The Spirit learns, via the life force of plants and animals, what it's like to be planted as a seed, develop and sprout, and become part of the natural order; it also learns what it's like to be sacrificed as food so that other life may continue.

So, the Spirit cares deeply about the well-being of all creatures and strives for global peace and harmony."

God In Hoodoo

Despite the common assertion that Hoodoo is a magic system rather than a religion, the vast majority of its practitioners are Christians. Two broad types of Christians engage in spiritual practice.

- Catholics and

- Protestants

Catholicism's foundation is Jewish. In fact, Jews, Christians, and Muslims all think of Abraham as a common ancestor, and both Jews and Christians respect the Old Testament. Christianity grew out of a Jewish movement that Jesus started, which was mostly made up of radical and liberal Pharisees. Christianity, as we know it today, came from a group of Jews who broke off to start their own religion. The following are only some of the many key distinctions between Judaism and Christianity:

- God as Trinity

- Original Sin

- Jesus as Messiah

- Concepts of Paradise and Hell

- The Papacy

Catholics who practice Papacy Hoodoo can pray to any deities, including the Holy Trinity, Mary, the Angels, and the Saints. A Catholic Hoodoo practitioner in a place like New Orleans, where Catholicism has been integrated into Voodoo beliefs and rituals, might also pray to the Voodoo gods.

During the Reformation, led by Martin Luthor, the Protestant Church separated from the Catholic Church in protest at Catholic teachings, practices, and hierarchical hierarchy. Luthor and other Reformers rejected the churches' teachings on free will, purgatory, and the sale of indulgences. Protestants believe that a direct connection with God is possible without an intermediary. In contrast, Catholics believe that a mediator (such as a priest) is required between God and man.

People raised in any Protestant tradition are likely to pray to the "Father, Son, and Holy Spirit" or "in the name of Jesus" when asking for anything spiritual. Some of these practitioners may direct prayers or pleas toward the devil, whose image may have fused with that of the deceiver-god of the crossroads. It's important to note that in these contexts, people often consider Satan and the devil to be two separate beings. They may also construct altars and pray to non-religious spirits and/or deities, as well as to the souls of the departed.

Death in hoodoo

Many root operators begin to deal with the deceased's spirits in the form of ancestors, the spirits of the dead tied to them by blood. It is thought that the deceased do not die but rather ascend to another dimension of existence, from which they may watch over and assist us. From this higher level, the ancestors may advise us in our everyday lives, intercede with the Divinity on our behalf, and defend us in times of need.

The process of working with the ancestors starts with the creation of an ancestral altar. Before I go any further, I want to stress that many of the root workers are Christians and adhere to God's word in Exodus 20:3 to "have no other gods before me." As a result, the rootworkers do not worship their ancestors because they adore them. This ceremonial adoration takes place at the ancestral altar. (See also The Ancestors.)

In other circumstances, a practitioner may visit the cemetery to ritually take soil from a specific tomb or tombs for use in spells and rituals. When getting dirt from a cemetery for spells and rituals, there are a few things to think about. Some of these factors include:

- the location of the cemetery;

- how the deceased died;

- obtaining permission; and

- where to acquire soil.

Also, the cemetery's dirt is not just taken; it is paid for after a ghost is consulted and a deal is made. Some practitioners consider working with the saints and saints of the people to be working with the dead since the saints were once alive human beings who also led unusually virtuous lives.

Working with non-Christian entities

While hoodoo is founded on the ideas and magical practices of numerous traditions (without their religious doctrine), it is nonetheless heavily inspired by Christianity and diverse African faiths. The practice of evocation involves the reverence of your ancestors, the commitment of the dead to work for you, the devil at the crossroads, powerful saints, and non-Christian creatures.

Some of these beings are deities linked with non-Christian faiths. Spiritual practitioners are often seen constructing altars and directing requests to deities from non-Christian pantheons:

• Hinduism

• Voodoo

• Pole

• Yoruba

• Santeria

For example, Ganesha is a popular non-Christian god seen in the Hoodoo tradition. He is often invoked to remove barriers, open the road, bestow good fortune, and bring the signatories riches.

Before petitioning a spirit or god outside of one's own culture or faith, it is vital to study how that culture worships and/or worships that deity, what sacrifices are suitable, and the deity's area of influence in the world. For example, if you wish to vanquish an opponent, you would not want to ask a god renowned for bestowing lovers. The education of these spirits/gods will enable you to approach them with your petition in a semi-traditional manner, honoring the culture's original beliefs and customs from whence that deity originated.

Spirits

In addition to the spiritual abilities stated above, numerous spirits do not necessarily fit into any of the previously named groups. These are some examples:

- Family spirits

- Plant and animal spirits

- Anthropomorphic spirits

Family spirits

While most people identify the word "family spirit" with the shapeshifting creatures said to have helped medieval witches, it may also allude to their brilliance or a kind of tutelary spirit. Other words for family spirit include Patron Saint, Guardian Angel, Daimon, and Most High Self. They serve as the protector and master of a person who often connects with humans via dreams and intuition.

Plant and animal spirits

The use of plants, minerals, and animal parts in the practice of magic is not unique to Hoodoo. Their usage is almost a universal phenomenon, and contemporary medicine owes much of its success to the ancient magicians' findings. Animism, the notion that spirits inhabit non-human beings, is central to Hoodoo's practice. When a radical practitioner employs a herb or a zoological oddity, such as a rabbit's foot, he recognizes the spirit that resides inside it. He might be asked to back his petition. (See also the Doctrine of Signatures.)

Anthropomorphic spirits

Anthropomorphism, often known as personification, is the practice of attaching human characteristics to inanimate objects or abstract concepts. The Anima Sola, or lonely soul, is a frequent anthropomorphic figure in the hoodoo, depicting a lady with shackles shattered between purgatory flames. She is frequently summoned to either deliver herself from misery or inflict pain on others. Other anthropomorphic spirits include Santa Muerte, who represents death as a holy spirit, and John the Conqueror, a well-known hero who embodies the qualities of the name's origin.

CHAPTER 5

Traditional Bone Reading

The reading of bones is a kind of divination in which animal bones, nuts, shells, and other oddities are used as dice or beads to get divine knowledge.

Each bone, or a portion of it, has a special meaning attributed to it, generally under the animal's features from which the bone is derived or the physical component represented by the bone. For example, since water buffaloes are migratory creatures, the water buffalo tooth is often connected with travel. For obvious reasons, the raccoon's penis bone is connected with sex and sexuality. Other things of symbolic importance, such as keys, horseshoe pendants, coins, roots, pyrite, and so on, may be incorporated.

Traditionally, bones were thrown in a circle drawn on the ground; however, contemporary bone readers prefer to toss them on an adequately designated fabric. This fabric may sometimes be animal skin, and this component of bone reading will be described in depth later.

All bone readers think that reading bones necessitate contact with the ancestors. Many readers have an Altar of the Ancestors where their bone sets are stored when not in use in a basket, a huge abalone shell, or a leather bag (called a "Bone Bag").

A solid connection with one's ancestors is critical since the soothsayer's ancestors, spirits, and guides communicate through the bones, not the soothsayer himself. As a result, each reading should begin with a prayer to the Ancestors for wisdom and guidance.

Getting Bones

The simplest and quickest way to get bones for divination is to purchase a set online from a reliable vendor. Such bone sets are typically considered ready to use as they are, but they are also regarded as a "beginning set," Many individuals often add more components to their set as they remove them. As a result, all sets for reading bones are different.

Some individuals like to acquire and construct their bone sets gradually. These folks often discover the bones on nature hikes, gently pick them off the street, or keep the bones of animals they have eaten. These people believe that finding, drying, and ritually preparing their bones imbues them with their energy and transforms them into a far more personal instrument. Suffice it to say animals are NEVER murdered specifically to obtain their bones for use in a bone reading set. Objects such as dice, beads, pendants, and so on may be readily bought at ten-cent stores, but oddities can also be added to your bone collection from old jewelry, unused keys, and other items you already have at home.

I have three bone reading sets in my possession. The first was an online starter set that developed to include additional bones that I added over time while removing or losing others. The second bone-reading set I have was similarly bought online and billed as a "travel kit." It has little bits that may easily fit into a small jar.

My third bone reading set was created by myself (see below). I designed this set with much research and experience with bone reading and other divination methods like tarot, Lenormand, and astrology. In addition, my bone set was inspired by the spirits of my ancestors, who talked with me via dreams and signs, and when I was working with other bone sets. When it came time to make this set, I knew I wanted to utilize individual pieces that were around the same size and form. I chose chicken bones because they were readily available and because birds have traditionally been connected with ceremonial sacrifice and cleaning in myths and customs.

Some bone readers, like tarot card readers, may choose to read their bones upright or inverted. Those bones that fall in an upright posture are anticipated to be positive, indicating that energy or condition is there and expanding; those that fall in a reversed position indicate that the energy of the bone is weakened or diminishing.

When recalling bones, pick a bone with two different sides to decide whether it is upright or inverted. Alternatively, you may mark the bones to identify which side is the head and which is the tail. I suggest using a plus sign (+) for heads and a negative sign (-) for tails or just painting or drawing a dot on one end of the bone to symbolize heads.

When the bone falls headfirst, it indicates good fortune; when it falls tail first, it represents ill fortune. As a reader, you must decide whether to include reversals in your readings and how to identify whether a bone is straight or upside down.

Blessing And Using Bones

Your bones should be sanctified and consecrated before usage. Each bone should be washed under cold running water, dried, dabbed with Florida Water, and burnt in incense.

Finally, each bone should be delivered to your ancestors and explained to them. This creates a "language" between you and your ancestors or spirit guides. When not in use, your bones should be placed at your Ancestor Altar in your bone bag or bone basket.

As previously stated, bones were once flung about a circle created on the ground. On the other hand, modern bone readers are more likely to toss them on a carefully marked fabric. A circle split into four equal quadrants is a frequent motif. This fabric is sometimes made from an animal's skin. You may still toss the bones in a circle made of soil if you like.

Like other divination techniques, many bone readers establish their own style and reading procedures while adhering to some commonly acknowledged divination system principles. As a result, no two bone readers read bones in the same manner, particularly considering that there is no standard set of reading bones. To summarize, there is no correct method to read bones, no guidelines, and even the bone reader may modify the way it reads bones every time they are melted.

When you initially learn to toss the bones on your casting cloth, you must experiment with them to establish the optimal distance to hold them on top of the fabric before releasing them. If you are too near to the fabric, they may not spread enough; if you are too far away, they may spread excessively, and the fall may cause bone injury in rare situations. You will achieve a good balance with practice.

When bones are melted, they may be interpreted in various ways. Options include, but are not limited to, left-to-right orientation.

Left to right orientation.

The bones on the left symbolize the past, the bones in the center represent the present, and the bones on the right represent the future or the outcome. It should be noted that bones that fall beyond the circle or reading surface are deemed "out of play" and are typically not read.

Separation from the reader

The bones are tossed in this instance, and those closest to the reader reflect the past. Those a bit farther away reflect the present, while those further out indicate future possibilities.

Orientation that is not linear

When interpreted from a non-linear viewpoint, the bones are tossed as before, but they are read without regard for any idea of a timeline (i.e., the bones on the left represent the past, the bones on the right represent the future, and so on). The bones are read as a whole and individually, and the spirit directs the reader as to the message, time, and so on...

Reading Surface & How To Read

Some readers might consider each section of the circle to symbolize a different aspect of life. The ringed cross, split into four quadrants, may indicate love, money, health, or the unknown.

These reading surfaces are different. In certain circumstances, they may be painted or embroidered on mats. Furthermore, the manner the surface is designated might differ substantially. A giant astrological wheel (a circle split into 12 sectors reflecting the signs/houses of the zodiac, which in turn symbolize many spheres of life) is a popular and widely used approach. The reading cloth is not confined to a circle, as seen in the picture on the left. You are not bound to utilize an astrological wheel to mark each region of the reading cloth; as long as the decision is made before the bones are cast, you are free to do so.

Some bone readers like to read their bones on an animal's tanned and preserved skin. The skin may be from the same animal or type of animal as the bones the reader uses for his or her bone reading sessions, although this is not always the case. Many bone reading sets now include bones from several animal species.

In certain circumstances, the animal in issue may be one with whom the bone reader has a connection or affinity; for example, it may symbolize personal or familial totemic energies, although this is not always the case. The option to use an animal's skin to toss one's own bones on, as well as the sort of animal to utilize, is a personal choice that the bone reader must make.

The position of the bones

When bones are cast on animal skin, the part of the body on which the bones settle may be evaluated since it can identify the area of life to which the bones' message alludes. As an example:

- The head - Bones that fall on this place will offer an idea or indication of the seeker's present attitude or ideas about the query he puts to the bones.

- The Neck - The head is the crown of the body, but the neck has the ability to swivel its head in whatever direction it wants; thus, the bones that fall here symbolize external elements that impact the person or the circumstance.

- The Chest - Because the chest region surrounds the heart, the bones that fall here symbolize the person's sentiments about their circumstances, which may or may not be the same as their thinking. This section also includes the heart's desire and, in many cases, the true motive.

- The left front paw - The term "left" derives from the Latin word for "left," The bones that fall here signify the power of resistance working against the seeker, if any.

- The left hind leg - This section deals with the past and the forces and influences that have shaped history.

- The right front paw - The bones that fall here suggest what is essential or needed to handle their issue or problem to stay on the "correct road." This section also shows their allies and aids.

- The right hind leg - This location reflects the situation's future or conclusion.

- The groin region is all about sex and sexuality. It also indicates recurring patterns of thinking and behavior, which might be beneficial or harmful.

- Because the tail covers the anus, which is where waste departs the body, the bones that fall here represent the lesson(s) that may be derived from this scenario.

Bone Friction

Bone friction is a technique used by some bone readers, but not all. It entails interpreting patterns in which bones fall regardless of the unique significance of the bone itself.

When a bone reader notices such patterns, it is one of the first things the reader looks at before analyzing the individual bones and their connections. Scanning bones is incredibly intuitive, and it is thought that the bones' spirit guides it. The following are some examples of popular models:

- Vertical triangle - When bones create a vertical triangle, it symbolizes that something is growing and manifesting. The triangle's bones represent what is developing or expressing.

- Inverted triangle - An inverted triangle indicates that some influence or situation is waning.

- T-Shape - This pattern represents bricks. One bone's energy is impeding the energy of another.

- Parallel Lines - Bones that form parallel lines (like an equal sign) suggest that the energies represented by the bones are in equilibrium.

- X - Shape- The bones that form an X suggest a strong desire; depending on what they are, the bones that comprise this pattern may work together or against each other.

- Vertical lines - Vertical lines have a macho and energetic feel to them. They reflect a positive response.

- Horizontal lines - These are feminine and receptive lines. They are a negative response.

- Diagonal lines are used to symbolize separation. Examine the bones on both sides to see what is separating.

- Horseshoe: When the bones form a U-shape or horseshoe, they signify good fortune, but when the U is turned upside down, it signifies terrible fortune.

In certain circumstances, the bones may indicate particular symbols, such as a desk, a vehicle, or a tree, with little creativity. Such symbols are interpreted in these instances based on your comprehension. An automobile, for example, may indicate movement (the direction in which the car is moving); or a tree may signify steady growth, and so on.

The Ritual

The practice of divination incorporates ceremony and/or ritual components. The fundamental process is as follows:

Pose a query.

Shake the bone bag or the bone basket to randomize the oracle.

Melt the Oracle by tossing or plucking the bones from the bone bag.

Interpret the outcomes.

Aside from that, the reader might tailor his or her ritual to their preferences. Rituals are significant because they have significance and power for the people participating. When done correctly, they work as triggers to awaken intuition and put the reader's mind in a receptive condition, which favors the success and accuracy of divination.

When not used, the bones are preserved in a leather bag, my bag of bones, and maintained on the Ancestors' Altar. They may be kept between treatments in a big abalone shell designed for this purpose. I light a candle on my Altar of the Ancestors, place a clear glass of water on it, and ignite some incense as part of my bone reading routine. I ask my forefathers for wisdom and guidance. Then I take the bone bag and the casting cloth from the altar and place them on a table to be read. In certain circumstances, though, I may place the casting cloth on the floor in front of the altar and hurl them there.

When I'm reading the bones for someone else, I have them sit in front of me with the casting cloth between us. I offer them the bone that belongs to their species to hold in my hand as a symbol. If they identify as males,

I force them to grasp Adam's bone; if they identify as women, I force them to hold Eve's bone. I tell them to shut their eyes and focus on the subject or problem they want to learn more about. I tell them that they must lay the bone in the middle of the fabric when they are ready.

While contemplating their issue or problem, I gather the twelve remaining bones in my hands. I quietly request that my ancestors speak with the searching ancestors and send us the answers we need to handle their problem or inquiry. When the client sets the bone on the cloth and says it is ready, I take the other 12 bones in my hands and instruct them to breathe on the bones (essentially by breathing their question into the bones). The bones are then thrown onto the fabric.

When I'm through, I place the bones in the bone bag and reinstall them on the Ancestors Altar. The light, together with the water, stays on the altar as a gift of appreciation to the Ancestors for their aid.

Connection to the bones

The bones are read regarding where they fall inside the circle and in relation to each other when tossed. As a result, the significance of a bone in reading might grow, contract, or otherwise change based on its connection to the other bones.

On the right side of the fabric, for example, the man's bone next to the large bone may presage contact with a guy who will give you a job. On the bottom left side of the cloth, the love bone adjacent to the evil eye bone may represent prior harm from a failed relationship that impacts the client's current circumstances.

Other examples are:

- Spirit Bone + Eve Bone = A spiritual woman possessing great

- wisdom and intuition.

- Bone of the Evil Eye + Bone of Adam = A jealous man.

- Earth Bone + Eve Bone = Pregnancy

- Bone of Fire + Bone of Eve = A woman with a fiery temperament, a red head

- Heart bone + Adam's bone = a loving man.

- Bone of the Evil Eye + Bone of the Pyramid = financial loss, job loss, unemployment.

- Bone of the Evil Eye + Bone of the Earth = physical illness, illness, bad health

- Evil-eye bone + Horseshoe bone = Bad luck, difficulty

- Air Bone + Eve Bone = A woman with an air head. A blonde woman

- Pyramid Bone + Evil Eye Bone = A deal is late.

- Heart Bone + Water Bone = A "cool" ratio.

- Spirit Bone + Cross Bone = Spirits are with you. Your wish will be granted.

Again, if we think of time as a linear force that moves forward from left to right, we must analyze the sequence in which the bones fall when they are adjacent to one another. For example, if Adam's Bone falls to the left of the Spirit's Bone, man will seek the Spirit for assistance. He pursues his spirituality and spiritual things. If we reverse this and move the Spirit's Bone to the left of Adam's bone, the spirits follow man, speak with him, give him signals, and so on.

Some individuals may find the interpretation of bones scary at first, so they may choose to begin with simple approaches and graduate with more complex methods of tossing bones as they develop.

Bone reading is a skill that takes time to learn. It is a long-consuming procedure, depending on how much time and effort you put into the art and your "dowry" in divination. It is essential to begin with, some fundamental strategies to improve the divinatory talents you may create.

Drawing every day

A simple method to include bone reading into your daily routine is to draw a bone randomly from your bag or bowl of bones and read it as a theme for the day. Look for indicators of the bone's message or energy in the people you encounter and the events that occur throughout the day. Please keep track of your daily extractions in a bone journal so you can review them afterward.

As you grow more comfortable with this technique, you should reach into your bag/bone bowl, take a few bones randomly, and toss them onto the reading surface. Examine the bones before you, choose a model that speaks to you, and enter your prediction(s) in your bone journal to assess your correctness or inaccuracy. When you're comfortable with this method, you may broaden your bone reading exercise by tossing all the bones at once. Again, dividing the configuration into discrete groups and reading them independently may be beneficial.

Yes / No Answer Divination

Except for Adam and Eve's bones, remove all bones from the bag of bones in which they are housed. Reach inside the sack without peeking and take out one bone while thinking about your question. If you pick Adam's bone (White), the answer is yes; if you choose Eve's bone (Black), the answer is no.

Another way is selecting a bone that reflects the object of your inquiry. While you consider your question, hold this bone in your non-dominant hand (left hand for right-handed people and right hand for left-handed individuals). When ready, toss the bone randomly onto the casting cloth. The answer is affirmative if the bone falls more vertically; nay, if the bone falls horizontally.

Three bone extractions are required to address an issue or difficulty.

Consider your question and, one at a time, pick three bones from the bone bag and arrange them in a straight line in front of you.

- The first bone signifies your issue or issue.

- The second bone indicates what is needed to remedy the issue or problems.

- The third bone represents the most probable result if the bones' counsel is followed.

Techniques ranging from intermediate to advanced

Combining divination techniques

Conjure's bones constitute a full oracular divination method. Some readers, however, choose to mix bones with other divination techniques to offer a new depth to their readings. We've previously seen how some readers use bones to spin an astrological wheel; in this part, we'll look at how bones may be mixed with other divination techniques.

Tarot cards

Another method of divination is the tarot. It is a system based on 78 cards split into 22 major arcana and 56 minor arcana. The Major Arcana often relate to topics of lofty significance or deep goals, while the Minor Arcana are concerned with earthly concerns, with daily existence. Simply put, the cards in a card game are managed by shuffling and distributing them. Each position in a spread has its own designation (for example, the past, future, hopes, fears, and so on), and the card that falls in that place is interpreted in reference to that description.

You have two options when combining bone reading with a tarot reading. They are as follows:

Pull a bone randomly from the bone bag or basket and lay it over the tarot card in a tarot spread. The connotations of the tarot card and the bone are discussed, and an interpretation is provided.

Reach inside your bone basket once again and take a few random bones to scatter throughout the area. The bones are read in conjunction with the tarot cards to determine where they fall on or near the tarot cards.

The same method(s) may be used for other card-based divination systems like Lenormand and Playing Cards.

Conclusion

We've seen how hoodoo practitioners use African folk magic, but they often call on Catholic saints or biblical figures like Moses to assist them in casting spells. In reality, most hoodoo practitioners are Catholics who believe in Catholic saints and African gods. Hoodoo sessions in the United States are held in English, and hoodoo practitioners pronounce their "magic."

The practitioner will use roots, herbs, crystals, animal parts, and sometimes even the person's own tears, saliva, urine, and other bodily fluids to do the session. A practitioner will almost certainly use text from the Bible's book of Psalms, but the session will not be done in the name of Jesus. Instead, he or she will ask the saints or other people for advice on how to use the roots and other talismans used in the rite. He needs documentation to pass along since hoodoo is not a religion. On the other hand, practitioners pass on their abilities to their successors.

Many adherents of both faiths think that Voodoo was the first religion. Hoodoo became a denomination in the same way that Methodists, Lutherans, Baptists, and other Protestant Christian churches have. Although most people dismiss voodoo and hoodoo as simple superstitions, a sizable community, mainly in the southern United States, sincerely believes in one of these belief systems. I hope you liked this book, and good luck with your studies!

www.ingramcontent.com/pod-product-compliance
Lightning Source LLC
LaVergne TN
LVHW010343200726
843507LV00010B/1632